Krazy Faith

Stories of Miracles, Signs, and Wonders

Maxine Arlene Ryan

ISBN-13: 978-09911888-0-2
ISBN-10: 0991188802

Library of Congress Control Number: 2013920546

Printed in the United States of America

Dedication

To Robert L. Ryan Jr., I dedicate this book to you. You are an incredible, humble, caring, loving man of God. I wouldn't be here without your unconditional love and support. Thank you so much. Carisha and Amari, Mommy loves you!

To my mom, Pamela McGusty, thank you for always being there for me. Your encouraging words and support mean so much to me. I would not be here without you. I love you Mom!

To Rachel Brown, Mama, thank you for your prayers, support and believing in me. I love you!

Thanks to my mentor, Pastor Paula Hazel. You are a true inspiration to me. Your Proverbs 31 lifestyle is a powerful example. Thanks for always being there to pray with me and encourage me! Thanks for allowing the Holy Spirit to lead you. I love you!

Last, but not least, to Vioda December, who was a true woman of faith. Because of your prayers, I stand here today. You have left a legacy in our hearts that we will cherish forever. We are deeply touched by your love. I miss you Granny. I love you!

Table of Contents

Introduction

For over ten years, my mother-in-law, Rachel Brown, told me to write down my testimonies because she saw potential for a book. Every time God performed a miracle, she would ask, "Maxine, are you writing this down? That's a book!" Actually, every time she would ask, I would question my ability to be a writer. I always thought my writing skills had to be perfect in order to become an author. I thought there was no possible way I could write down anything and share it with the world; but I knew the world needed to hear about what God had demonstrated through my faith. In fact, I knew God would use it for His glory. I just didn't know how He would use it. I also knew my grammar wasn't nearly where it should be, so I was uncomfortable with the thought of God using me to write anything.

When I was in college, I went to the writing center often. One day, the professor was looking over one of my papers. She was appalled at the way I often forgot to place an S on the end of several verbs in my sentences when it was necessary. I left that writing lab with tears in my eyes. As I walked out of the door, my husband, who attended the same college, was waiting for me. I said, "Baby, there is no way God will use me to write anything." He encouraged me, by saying, "Forget about what she is saying. You can do it." I looked at him in disbelief because I knew for sure God definitely had the wrong person. There was no way on this earth God could possibility use somebody like me. I thought again, Why would God want to use somebody that could hardly speak straight and who didn't have the ability to do anything in writing?

One day, I was on a weekday morning prayer line that was birthed out of Bishop T.D. Jakes' 2012 Woman Thou Art Loosed Conference. A prophecy came through the WTAL line corporately. The woman who was prophesying said God would use some of the women on the prayer line to write books. To be honest, I didn't even allow it to get into my spirit because I was already convinced that there was no way God would use me in that capacity. No way! Not long after that, I was on the phone with my cousin Pastor Paula Hazel, and she started praying for me. She stopped in the midst of her prayers and after speaking in the tongues, said, "A book, a bestseller book." My eyes sprang wide open and so did my mouth. I was in awe. For the first time, I knew God was speaking directly to me. God revealed to me that I would write a best-selling book. I felt as though a light clicked on in my spirit.

It was hard to imagine how I was going to start, but I knew if God said it, His grace was enough to take me through it. I hung up the phone, feeling humbled by the fact that God would use me like this. If that was not confirmation enough, that very evening my pastor (Senior Pastor Dale O'Shields of Church of

the Redeemer; Gaithersburg, MD) challenged the congregation
to do twenty-one days of consistent Bible reading. The
congregation read the book of St. John. That very day, I was on
chapter 21 of the book of John. I was reading the last two verses
of chapter 21 when something blew my mind: John 21: 24, 25
(MSG). It reads: *This is the same disciple who was eyewitness to
all these things and wrote them down. And we all know that his
eyewitness account is reliable and accurate. There are so other
things Jesus did. If they were all written down, each of them, one
by one, I can't imagine a world big enough to hold such a
library of books.*

Screaming Hallelujah! Words could not explain the way I
felt after reading these two verses. My mother-in-law's voice
came alive in my spirit so clearly, but I heard the Holy Spirit's
voice the loudest. I felt blessed that God would want to use
someone who couldn't speak or write to bring Him glory. I
realized all of my pain and shortcomings weren't about me, but
to bring glory to my Creator, the very source of my life. I
realized I wasn't going to write this book. The Holy Spirit that
lives on the inside of me was going to write this book. I pray
right now, in the name of Jesus, that God of our Lord Jesus
Christ, the Father of glory, may give you the spirit of His
wisdom and revelation in the knowledge of Him. I pray that your
eyes of understanding will be enlightened (see Ephesians 1:17-
18). I decree and declare that you will overcome by the blood of

the lamb, and the words of my testimonies (see Revelation 12:11). I pray right now that you will develop a deeper relationship with the Savior (The Anointed One) or you will come to know God as your personal Savior, in the name of Jesus! Amen!

Chapter 1
God Still Performs Miracles

A miracle is "an effect or extraordinary event in the physical world that surpasses all known human natural powers and is ascribed to supernatural cause" (dictionary.com). A miracle is a supernatural thing that only God can do; believers can also perform miracles through the manifestation of the Holy Spirit (see 1 Corinthians 12:7).

In March of 2013, my sister Simone called with some horrifying news. Our little cousin Jadon had been rushed to the emergency room. I could tell by the urgency in her voice that it was serious. Jadon lives in my home country, Guyana, South America. Guyana is a poor third world country. Health and medical systems need tremendous improvement. My sister told me he had to be transported to another hospital because the hospital in the small village where I grew up could not do anything else to assist him. When I received the call from my sister, I was about to step inside of a grocery store, but I paused and began praying in the Holy Spirit. I needed the Holy Spirit to lead me through how to pray in this situation and what to pray for. My sister did not know what led up to Jadon's hospitalization, so I didn't want to pray amiss. The store didn't have what I was looking for, so I walked out hurriedly about two minutes later. As soon as I made my way back to my vehicle, my son, who was sitting in the passenger seat, knew something had occurred because of my facial expressions. After I explained everything to him, I continued praying.

One thing I have learned about prayer is that it's so important to be led by the Holy Spirit in every situation. When I am unsure of what to pray, I tap into the Holy Spirit and wait until He speaks. I continued praying in the Holy Spirit while driving and the Holy Spirit laid it on my heart to pray for my little cousin who, at that moment, was in an ambulance on a 45-minute ride to another hospital. In my country, ambulances are not as equipped as those in America. They are not equipped to handle every situation; but I knew my God was well able to handle every situation that presented itself.

I began praying, calling on the God of Abraham, Isaac and Jacob. I began interceding, asking God to dispatch angels to intervene in that ambulance! I said, "Angels of God, I command you to go into that ambulance right now and touch Jadon in the name of Jesus." Even though I did not know for sure what was going on thousands of miles away, I knew God was listening and that He would answer my prayers. When I finally made my way home, I called my Aunt Juliet and we began calling on the God of my grandmother, declaring Jadon would live and not die. When I finished praying with my aunt, I called on the warriors and intercessors by posting a plea for prayer for Jadon on the WTAL social network page. I had warriors praying all over the United States.

A day later, I found out that a miracle had taken place. I found out my little cousin had not been feeling well, so his parents took him to the hospital. When he arrived, he was in pain, so the doctors gave him morphine. I am not sure why this little boy was given morphine, but his body completely shut down. He was non-responsive; in fact, his parents thought they had lost him. He was slipping in and out of consciousness. They rolled my little cousin's lifeless body into the ambulance--unsure of the outcome.

But God had heard some praying women. Jadon started responding to his mother's touch and her voice as she called out to him in the ambulance. Glory to God! I believe without a doubt that the angels of the Lord were present in that ambulance. That lifeless body suddenly moved because God heard some praying women and took control of the situation. Prayer works! Within twenty-four hours, my little cousin started moving and talking in his hospital room. The doctors and nurses were in awe because, according to them, he had suffered a stroke. All of this happened on a Friday; by Sunday morning, Jadon was totally restored. He was moving and speaking normally. Monday morning, Jadon was discharged from the hospital. He would have been discharged sooner, but in my country, patients do not get discharged from the hospital on the weekend.

If you are going through a situation and you need a miracle, just call on the God of Abraham, Isaac and Jacob. He is well able to deliver you. God still performs miracles!

Chapter 2
What is Faith?

Above all, faith is totally committing, trusting, and
believing God's Word. It is an outward display of confidence in
the Word of God. Faith is the responsibility of a believer to
believe in the finished work of Jesus Christ. We must believe
that regardless of what we might be facing today, we have
already overcome it. Faith expresses itself by love. This kind of
love is called agape love, which was demonstrated over two
thousand years ago when Jesus died on the cross for the
redemption of sin. It is not an emotion.

Faith has no limits; there is *nothing* it cannot produce. It is
the firm belief in, knowing and acting on the Word of God. It is
the belief that, without reservation or doubt, what God said is

solid, valid and real. Dr. Creflo Dollar, (Senior Pastor of World Changers Church International) says, "Faith is not trying to get God to do something; it is a positive response to what grace has already made available." We already have all of the spiritual blessings we need for life and Godly-living; but we have to, by faith, transfer it from the spiritual realm to the natural realm. Faith is a muscle according to Apostle Guillermo Maldonado of King Jesus Ministry in Miami. Faith grows over time when it is tried and tested. We can move from having a small size of faith to having a large measure of faith.

The word faith in the Greek language is *elpis*, which means to anticipate, usually with pleasure, expectation, or confidence, faith and hope. The Hebrew word for faith is *emcun*, which means to establish trust and trust-worthiness. Hebrews 11:1 says, *Now faith is the substance of things hoped for, the evidence of things not seen.* When you ask God in prayer and faith, you receive what you have prayed for immediately after saying, "Amen." It is impossible to please God without faith because anyone who comes to Him must believe that He exists and that He rewards those who earnestly seek Him (see Hebrew 11:6). If we have faith, even as small as a mustard seed, we can say to any mountain, "Move from here to there," and it will be moved. Nothing shall be impossible for us (see Mathew 17:20). A mustard seed is the smallest of all seeds, but it becomes the largest of garden plants; it grows into a tree, and birds come in it and make their nests in its branches (see Matthew 13:32). God has given every believer a personalized measure of faith, but when we exercise our faith, it grows over time. Faith comes when we constantly hear God's word. If we are not exposed to the word of God, we will not have the God kind of faith. So it is safe to say, no word, no faith. More word, more faith. Also, the word of God (faith) is spirit and life, according to John 6:63. When we accept Jesus Christ as our personal Savior, we move from death to life. The spirit of the Father is dwelling on the inside of every born again. When we speak faith (God's word) out of our mouths, we bring life to any and every situation we are facing.

Joshua 1:8 says, *This book of the law shall not depart out of thy mouth; but thou shalt mediate therein day and night, that thou mayest observe to do according to all that is written therein: for then thou shalt make thy way prosperous, and then thou shalt have success.* When we mediate day and night on the word of God, we grow in our faith and faith is easily spoken through our mouths. Faith by itself does not work if it is not accompanied by action. If we have faith without work, this kind of faith is dead (see James 2:17). According to the Merriam-Webster dictionary, faith is: A firm belief in something for which there is no proof. It is having complete trust. Everyone has faith in something, but our very first experience with the God kind of faith is when we make the decision to accept Jesus Christ as our personal Savior. Faith is a gift to mankind, and it cannot be earned. Our Heavenly Father gives it to us, and we cannot do anything to deserve this gift. It is not because of us that we have it; it is purely because of who God is. Ephesians 2: 8-9 (KJV) tells us, *For by grace are you saved through faith; and that not of yourselves: it is the gift of God: Not work, lest any man should boast.* Therefore, by faith, I believe that Jesus Christ is the foundation of my faith. He is the chief cornerstone of my salvation (see Ephesians 2:20).

By faith, I humbly accept what Jesus did for me on the cross. He died and rose again on the third day (Matthew 27:63). By faith, I am truly thankful for the blood that was shed to take away my sins (Roman 6:11). By faith, I confess Jesus Christ is the Alpha and Omega, the first and the last, the beginning and the end (Revelation 22:13). By faith, I believe, He is the Wonderful Counselor, Mighty God, Eternal Father, and that He is the Prince of Peace (Isaiah 9:6). By faith, I believe that Abraham, Isaac and Jacob served God, and they each had an intimate relationship with Him. By faith, I believe that they heard about the promise, but I get to live the promise. By faith, I believe that Jesus Christ lives in my heart as my Comforter (John 14:16). By faith, I believe I am no longer empty, alone, worthless or insecure. I no longer have wounds.

By faith, I believe that God transformed my life. By faith, I believe I am restored to the very image and likeness of my

Father. By faith, I believe the kingdom of God dwells within me, and I share in the glory of God with Jesus Christ himself (Roman 8:17). By faith, I believe I am fearfully and wonderfully made; and I am the apple of God's eyes (Psalms 139:14). By faith, I believe my past is behind me and I have a great future in God. By faith, I have received God's promises that He made to my forefather Abraham, my father of faith. I have received it with gladness and humbleness. I am an heir to the promise because I accepted Jesus Christ as my personal Savior. By faith, I allow God's Word to move me from glory to glory (Galatians 3:29). By faith, I can truly say, the Lord is the real reason that I live, and I am alive to bring glory to His name (2 Corinthians 3:18). Jesus Christ is the lover of my soul. He is the very reason I am able to breathe and have my being. Without God, I am truly nothing!

Apostle Leroy Thompson, Sr. (Ever Increasing Word of Life Christian Center, Darrow, LA) said, "When we make a demand, God makes a command from heaven. When we activate our faith here on earth, God can release His supernatural powers to change our natural situations. God Has placed himself on the line where our faith on the earth will control Him. Believers have the ability to access the Kingdom of God when we use our faith, at any given time." That's why the Bible says it's impossible to please our Father without faith and that is why He has commanded His children to live – in, with, and by faith. Faith is all the cash we need to see miracles, signs and wonders in our lives. It is Heaven's currency. Faith will move mountains; faith will cause favor to fall into our laps. The blind beggar in Luke 18 knows all about this. He made a demand by using his faith, even when the people asked him to be quiet. He pushed forward, calling out to the Son of David. He made a demand. In the end, because of his faith, heaven made a command and he received his sight.

Our entire Christian journey revolves around –the fact that we are created by God to live by faith, and we must believe in Him by faith. If we can see what we are believing God for with our naked eyes, faith is not present. Second Corinthians 4:18 says, *While we look not at the things which are seen, but at the things which are not seen: for the things which are seen are temporal; but the things which are not seen are eternal.* Hebrews 11:1 says, *Now faith is the substance of things hoped for, the evidence of things not seen.* The word *now* in this verse means without further delay. Therefore, the minute we pray, we must believe we have whatever we are asking for. We are directed to commit, trust and rely on God's ability, not our own.

When I first received Christ as my personal Savior, my pastor always said, "If only we can walk through something without giving up. In the end, victory would be sweet, and we would never have a reason to turn back. Our lives after that would not be the same." Looking back on those words, I can see that what he said is true. My very first experience after accepting Christ as my personal Savior really tested my faith in God. I was stripped of everything that I built up with my own strength. God brought me to a place where I had no other choice but to trust, rely and commit myself to Him.

I was a single mother at that time, and had recently moved from Brooklyn, New York to Virginia Beach to live with my sister who was in the military. God drew me away from Brooklyn to Virginia Beach because He knew my life would change. While still living in Brooklyn, I started feeling uncomfortable and having a strong desire to move. Everything about the way I was living felt uncomfortable and out of place. I wore revealing clothing and went to nightclubs, but I felt the urgency to change and give my life to God. My son was two years old, and I had a strong desire to do better for him. I remember walking down Flatbush Avenue in Brooklyn, feeling suddenly naked. I felt like I literally did not have any clothes on. I felt emptiness and loneliness, and I felt like something was missing in my life.

God opened the door, then I moved to Virginia Beach. My sister was not saved at that time. When I moved, I had an immediate strong need to find a church home. Moving was not easy at all. I was a single mother with no child support in sight, no car and no job. I had to depend on my sister for everything. Eventually, I started receiving food stamps and two hundred dollars a month in support, but that wasn't nearly enough to buy everything my son and I needed. I didn't know anything about depending on God, even though I heard about it from family members. I had no idea what that looked like. Even though I was born into a Christian background, it was just something I heard. I went to God occasionally when I was in trouble, but He wasn't the Lord of my life at that time.

My sister occasionally attended a small church. We went one Sunday morning and God used this small ministry to change my life. True Gospel church was awesome and this was the beginning of my journey as a Christian. The day that I committed my life to the Lord, the pastor made an altar call and I knew it was my day. I remember walking slowly up to the front of the church, with my legs shaking and tears flowing from my eyes. That day, I opened my heart to God and my life was *completely* transformed. I walked back to my seat, totally set free by the Son. I had given my heart to Christ before, but this time, it was different. I felt changed. Being a babe in Christ wasn't easy at all for me. I crept around the word, not even understanding what I was reading. The devil had a field day with me. He used my sisters against me a lot. Because I was a babe in Christ and did not know how much power I had through the word of God, it created a lot of disturbance in the home. The devil knew I was weak, so he used my sisters to tear me down. Many Sundays, I went to church in tears.

Looking back on some of those situations, I realize it was wasted time and energy, trying to fight with the flesh. I didn't realize the battle was not against my sisters; it was against the devil himself. I often wonder if I had lived a life of few words instead being a woman of prayer, if my sisters would have come to Christ sooner. In fact, I was so much on fire for the Lord that every time someone said, "Jesus!" I would break out in a shout and praise God. I was not pretending. It felt like fire shut up in my bones, and the very name of Jesus set me off like a light switch.

I walked around with a big green bible and I read the word everywhere I went. I didn't understand anything about witnessing and loving people regardless of their sins. I used the word of God to condemn my sisters because their lives were contrary to what God's word said. Because I used the word to rip my sisters into pieces, we grew further apart.

This behavior got worse when I had a dream of a man laying his hands on me. When he put his hands on me, my body started shaking out of control. There was a group of women standing around me, trying to calm me down. But they couldn't even touch me because the fire that was on me couldn't be calmed down. I lifted my head up in the dream and the man's face was blank. He didn't have a face. After having this dream, the Holy Spirit inside of me got stronger and I walked around shouting and pointing fingers at everyone whom I thought wasn't living according to the word of God. The wedge between my sisters and I got wider and wider.

I later realized that God did not want me to use His word to condemn my sisters or point my fingers at them. He wanted me to pray for them and love them unconditionally. While He did not want me to love their sin, He did want me to live my life right before them so I could be an example and of His love. The way I lived my life spoke louder than any words.

My son and I moved out of my sister's home and moved into a two-bedroom apartment. I only made minimum wage and struggled with whether to pay my tithes or my rent. As babes in Christ, we often do battle with the basic principles of the word of God. To be very honest, in the beginning I thought: *There is no way I am paying my tithes!* I thought God wanted me to take care of my son and me first. Then, I would sow my tithes from whatever was left. Through the ministry of Pastor Clinton Cuffee at Freedom by The Word Ministry, I learned that God required me to trust Him and pay my tithes first, and He would then take care of the rest. Paying tithes first brings honor to God, and it's a way for us to tell Him thanks for being the provider for us that he is. By faith, I started paying my tithes first, giving Him the first fruit of what I made. This wasn't easy, especially when I fell behind in my rent.

Then one Sunday at church, my pastor released a prophetic word, directed specifically to one person. He said, "God said this week, someone will be stripped of everything. But don't be dismayed; I will rebuild, thus saith the Lord." I didn't believe that word was for me. I even looked at the person on each side of me and said, "That person will need Jesus for sure."

Virginia Beach has very strict laws. One of them states that if you are late paying your rent three or more times within a certain period, the landlord has the right to evict you. That very week, I found out that the prophecy was for me. I came home from work Monday evening and found a notice on my door, stating that I had forty-eight hours to vacate my apartment. The notice also read that the landlord wanted to regain possession of the apartment. Even though God had told me in advance what was going to happen through His prophet, I was highly upset that God would do that to me. I felt as though I was living in a nightmare. I was hurt and frustrated. I felt rejected, speechless and sad. I was scared and in a state of panic. I started blaming myself for not doing everything in my power to prevent this from happening.

I felt like I had failed my son by not providing a roof over his head. However, as the week went by, God started showing me how much He loved and cared for me. My church family was incredible. The day of my move came very quickly. The pastor, along with his wife and several faithful members from my church, came to rescue me. Before I knew it, within two hours, my little two-bedroom apartment was totally packed up.

Everything I owned, beside clothes and personal belongings, was placed into storage. I felt the presence of the Lord in the midst of my situation. For the first time in my Christian life, God demonstrated His love to me by using His people. 1 John 4:18 suddenly came alive to me: *There is no fear in love; but perfect love casteth out fear.* I was afraid, but God showed up through His people and brought rest to my soul. He showed me how much He loved me by sending His people to show me love. I felt God holding my hands through the whole process. God fulfilled His promise to never leave me nor forsake me. Years later, when I applied for an apartment with my husband, my credit report did not show the eviction. God took care of it! If you are going through a situation right now that seems hopeless, know that it's not by accident that you are reading this book. Just like God came through for me, remember and take comfort in –knowing that He is no respecter of person. If He did it for me, He will do it for you. Keep pressing, keep calling God to His word, then stand still and see the salvation of the Lord! Give Him praise in the midst of it all.

I speak to every dead situation in your life right now. I decree in the name of Jesus that restoration will take place right now, in the name of Jesus! Thank God in advance for restoration!

After the eviction, I went back to live with my sister. I made up in my mind that I needed to live my life in pure faith, to rest, rely and commit myself to what God promised me through the man of God in prophecy. That wasn't easy, but I had the confidence that my faith in the Almighty would move me to bigger and better things, just like the man of God said. He would build me back up. I had to rest in His plan for my life.

Noah built an ark as God commanded him to do by faith. He had never seen rain according to Genesis 2:5. The word of God says, *For the Lord God had not caused it to rain upon the earth, and there was not a man to till the ground.* Even still, Noah was not responding to what he saw in the natural. He obeyed the voice of God and began building the ark by faith. He wasn't questioning what he heard, nor was Noah responding to what it looked like. Noah acted purely on what God told him to do. Noah had great faith. He trusted, believed and committed himself to do God's will. Can you imagine what the naysayers were saying when they saw Noah building the ark? They probably called him a fool and said, "Who does he think he is? There is no rain coming! Who does he think he is, saying he heard from God?"

Noah had what I call krazy faith.

This kind of faith is evident when everybody around you is saying how crazy it looks, but you know in your heart that God is leading you to do it. The world (and even some believers) won't understand this kind of faith. Krazy faith requires moving into the supernatural realm. To the naked eye, it looks crazy and impossible. Noah blocked out the naysayers and fixed his eyes on the promise. Noah did exactly what God commanded him to do. When he finished building the ark, he placed his family and two kinds of every animal, as God had commanded him, into the ark. Noah closed the door of the ark and waited until rain came. I imagine the naysayers sitting there laughing, saying how foolish Noah looked. However, God is faithful to keep His word. It rained for forty days and forty nights (see Genesis 7:12).

In addition, by faith, the woman with the issue of blood, as recorded in Mark 5:27, touched His garment and she was healed because of her leap of faith. She suffered for twenty years with constant bleeding. She had gone to several doctors over the years, had spent everything she had to pay them, but she didn't get better. Nevertheless, she heard about Jesus. So she came behind Him through the crowd and touched His robe. Immediately, the bleeding stopped and she could feel in her body that she had been healed of her troublesome condition.

Maybe you've been diagnosed with a life-threatening disease and doctors told you that you only have a short period of time left to live. There is yet hope for you. Jesus is passing by. – One touch, by faith, will change your life forever. One touch from the Master will turn your mourning into dancing. Reach out and grab your healing by faith now, and thank Him in advance for what He has done.

Chapter 3
God's Promise of Faith Fulfilled

I looked up the word faith in The Strong Concordance, a noted bible study tool. I was very surprised to learn that there were only two verses about faith in the Old Testament: one in Deuteronomy 32:20 and Habakkuk 2:4. God revealed to me that His promise of faith had yet to be fulfilled. God's promise of faith was to send His own son Jesus Christ to die. Then all who believe in Him would receive everlasting life. The Old Testament is the book of law, and the New Testament is about mercy and grace. Our forefathers lived under the old covenant. Most believers couldn't speak directly to the Father because the Advocate, Jesus Christ, had not yet walked on the earth as flesh.

The believers under this law met with God's presence at the Ark of the Covenant. Priests and prophets were the main communication between God and man. God also used different things such as a burning bush and a donkey to speak to mankind. Sacrifices were the main part of the covenant. The people of this law in the Old Testament earned a good reputation. They lived their lives in total obedience to God (see Hebrews 11:2).

Our forefathers heard about the promise of Jesus Christ, but did not get to see the promise of Jesus come to pass. They didn't get to experience the promise. Hebrews 11:13 (NLT) says, *Our forefathers died still believing what God had promise them. They did not receive what was promised, but they saw it all from a distance and welcomed it. They agreed that they were foreigners and nomads here on earth.* Abraham, Isaac and Jacob didn't live to see the promise of the Son come to pass. But we are blessed today to experience the promises of God.

In the New Testament, there are many verses about faith because the promise of faith had been fulfilled. Faith came and freed us from the law of sin and death. Now we are no longer bound under the law, but we live under grace and mercy. In Galatians 3:10-11(NLT), we find that *those who depend on the law to make them right with God are under a curse,* for *the Scriptures say, "Cursed is everyone who does not observe and obey all the commandments that are written in God's Book of Law."* Verse 11 says, *So it is clear that no one can be made right with God by trying to keep the law. For the Scriptures say, "It is through faith a righteous person has life."* We cannot be saved by obeying Moses' law. Galatians 3:2 reminds us that we can only be saved by believing and accepting the message we have heard about Jesus Christ.

Jesus Christ came and set us free from the law. He now lives in us. We were given a comforter. He leads and guides us through all truth. We are totally free from the law system. No longer will we have to sacrifice a burnt offering unto the Lord. The Son of Man came and set us free. The perfect Lamb was slain to take away the sins of the world. Every promise God made to the father of faith, Abraham, belongs to us. We are heirs to the promise because we belong to Christ. What was promised has been fulfilled, and we live in it and experience it today. The minute we accept Jesus Christ as our personal Savior, the promises are ours.

Most of the time, we don't know who we are in Christ. Because we do not know, we struggle in our faith in God. This struggle is representative of not understanding what the Son did when He came into this world. We struggle because we don't know who we are in Christ. We don't understand God's promises to Abraham and because we don't know, we don't live up to our full potential in God. We spend most of our Christian journey going through the motions, not receiving the promise. We live our lives in defeat and we spend years going around the same mountains, not realizing what God assured us of. We have the authority to speak to our mountain and tell it to move and, by faith, the mountain must do as we command it to do.

God has more for you. The best is yet to come in your life. Choose to believe the word of God by faith now, and your life will move to another level. The precious promise of faith was fulfilled by our Father, so no longer are we slaves to sin and death. Our salvation was bought with a price; we are bought with a price. Therefore, it's time to get in position by seeking God through the development of a daily prayer life and spending devotional time with God. It is in this position that God will reveal His plan for your life and you will move to your rightful place in Him. Your success comes from God, not from the things you possess. God wants to tell you things you have never known before. He wants to show you bigger and better things in His word. Make a decision right now to move higher in Christ. I call your life to be fruitful now in the name of Jesus. I speak life into your spiritual life. I decree that restoration will fall on you even now. Receive it by faith. Luke 3:9 (NLT) says, *Even now the ax of God's judgment is poised, ready to sever the roots of the trees. Yes, every tree that does not produce good fruit will be chopped down and thrown into the fire.*

Chapter 4
Confessing Words of Faith

In 2 Corinthians 4:13, it reads, *We having the same spirit of faith, according as it is written, I believed, and therefore have I spoken; we also believe, and therefore speak.* Confessing words of faith is an important tool that believers must employ in order to live a victorious life. Luke 6:45 says, *Out of the abundance of the heart the mouth speaks.* Whatsoever our hearts are filled with will come out of our mouths. When God created the earth, He spoke it into existence. So because we have the Spirit of God living in us, we too, have the authority to open our mouths and speak life into every circumstance.

Proverbs 18:21 says, *Death and life are in the power of the tongue: and they that love it shall eat the fruit thereof.* God's words are spirit and life (John 6:63). Whatsoever words we speak, whether they are of life or death, we will reap the fruit of them. Confessing words of faith is vital for Christians. Our speech determines the outcome of every situation. There was a period of time when the heat in my home would not work. I tried several times to turn it on, but no warm air would come out. This went on for about two or three days in the dead of winter.

One evening, my family and I were sitting around a table having bible study. I got real tired of being cold. I jumped up in outrage, laid my hand on the thermostat, and said, "In the name of Jesus, I command this heat to flow and this thermostat to work right now." My family, who was still sitting around the table, turned around and looked at me in amazement. After I was finished, I walked back over to the dining room table and before I could sit down, the heat kicked on. My house was filled with joyful noise after that. We started screaming and praising God for His goodness. Just that quick, God answered.

Psalm 119:11 tells us that we must hide God's word in our hearts that we may not sin against thee. If God's word is hidden in our hearts, it's easy for His word to flow out of our mouths during difficult times. What we say flows from what is in our hearts. If you want to know what's in a person's heart, just listen to what comes out of their mouth.

Believers have the authority to speak those things to be as though they were (see Romans 4:17). We can use our word to change any situation. A few years ago, my husband was active-duty military. He came home one day and said his working hours were going to change from days to nights. Immediately, I said, "That's not going to happen. I rebuke that in the name of Jesus." I wasn't rebuking my husband; I was rebuking any thought of an undesired shift change even getting into my spirit. My husband was originally doing a countdown to the shift change. Finally, he started announcing that there was one more week before his shift changed. I just kept speaking against it. I kept the faith, even when the devil told me otherwise. The day came when my husband's shift was supposed to change, but that very day, he received a call at home, saying they decided not to change the shift because they didn't have enough people to handle a split shift. I knew my words and prayers brought about the fruit of what I was declaring. Even when it looked like my husband's shift was about to change, I kept confessing what my desire was. When we speak and decree the word of God over our situations, things work out in our favor. Even though this seems small to most people, I believe we have the power to speak life and change the atmosphere in every situation.

During a really bad flu season, I was the only one in my family to catch the flu. I was confined in bed for many days, with the shakes, high fever, sweating, headache and body aching. Everyone that called me during this time said my family would also get the flu. Even while lying in my bed, sick as a dog, I declared that was not going to happen in the name of Jesus. I felt so sick that I told God there was no way I would want any one of my family members to go through that pain. Therefore, I guarded every phone call, making sure all of my words were positive. Then I covered my family with the blood of Jesus. As sick as I was, I started putting work to my faith. I got up one morning, still sick as a dog, took everything off my bed, put them into the washing machine, and went to war with Lysol spray. I sprayed everything everywhere, including my children's room; when I was finished spraying, still feeling weak, I crawled back into bed. I finally felt better a couple of days later, and then I started thanking God in advance for keeping my family members safe from the flu.

One morning, my son walked into the room, holding his head and he said, "Mommy, I think I have the flu." I said with all power and authority, "Oh no, I rebuke that thought in the name of Jesus. You do not have any fever, or any flu." He still wanted me to check his temperature. I checked it and just as I said, he had no fever. I gave him Tylenol for his headache and sent him on his way. Then, I opened my mouth again, declared and decreed that there was no sickness in his body in the name of Jesus. My test, however, was not over. The next day, my nephew came into my room and said, "Auntie, I think I have a fever." I said, "I rebuke that in the name of Jesus and I plead the blood of Jesus over that thought." Then, I placed my hand on his forehead and of course, he had no fever. When he left my room, I decreed that there would be no flu again in my home. No one else in my home became sick with the flu. I realized that if we accept the negative that people speak over us, then we will reap the fruits of it.

Start today by speaking life over dead situations and problems in your life. Most of all, speak God's word over your situation and you'll see miracles, signs and wonders take place before your very eyes. Even in situations that we consider small or unimportant, we can use our faith and our words to win every time. Matthew 25:21 (NLT) says, *You have been faithful in handling this small amount, so now I will give you many more responsibilities.*

Chapter 5
The Power of a Seed

Jesus Christ is the perfect seed that was given to mankind
for the redemption of sin. The word of God is the incorruptible
seed. It is the seed that will always produce a harvest; it will
never fail (see Luke 8:11). Every living thing begins with a seed.
The seed has the power to reproduce when it's sown into good
ground. Mathew 6:33 says, *But seek ye first the kingdom of God,
and his righteousness; and all these things shall be added unto
you.* Seeking the kingdom of God is most important of all. God
desires us to seek after His kingdom. He wants believers to have
an intimate relationship with Him because He is our very source
of life. In Matthew 13:4-8, (MSG) a farmer planted seeds. I see
the farmer as the pastor who preaches the word of God, which is
the seed of faith. *As he scattered the seeds, some of it falls on the*

road, and birds ate it. Some fell in the gravel; and sprouted quickly but didn't put down roots, so when the sun came up it withered just as quickly. Some fell in the weeds; as it came up, it was strangled by the weeds. Some fell on good earth, and produced a harvest. Here is how Jesus translated this parable in Matthew 13:18-23 (MSG): *When anyone hears the good news of the kingdom and doesn't take it in, it just remains on the surface, and so the Evil One comes along and plucks it right out of that person's heart. This is the seed the farmer scatters on the road. The seed cast in the gravel is the person who hears, and instantly responds with enthusiasm. But, there is no soil of character, and so when the emotions wear off and some difficulty arises, there is nothing to show for it. The seed cast in weeds is the person who hears the kingdom news, but weeds of worry and illusions about getting more and wanted everything under the sun strangle what was heard and nothing comes of it. Finally, the seed cast on good earth is that person who hears and takes in the news, and then produce a harvest beyond his wildest dreams.*

When harvest is produced, the word of God becomes flesh in our lives. Victory is produced when we take the word of God off the pages of the bible and apply it in our lives. When the farmer plants the seed, we take in God's word, place it in our hearts, and then and only then can fruit be produced. We have to protect and watch over this seed so that it isn't plucked out of the ground. When we believe and have knowledge of the word of

God, it is important for our growth and development as
believers. The more word we have hidden in our hearts, the
stronger we are in our faith. Romans 10:17 (NLT) says, *So faith
comes from hearing, that is, hearing the Good News about
Christ.* Hearing the word of God alone is not the only thing that
is required; we have to apply the word of God to our lives.
Applying the word of God means doing what it says.

James 1:22 (NLT) says, But d*on't just listen to God's word.
You must do what it says. Otherwise, you are only fooling
yourselves.* So let us cast our seed on good earth. When we hear
the word of God, and hide it in our hearts, when the devil comes
and tries to steal it, we can protect that seed by declaring the
word.

Jephthah knew the value of a seed, and he was faithful to
God. He kept his promises to the Lord. He was a great warrior in
Judges 11. He was born in disgrace because his mother was a
prostitute. Jephthah's half-brothers chased him away from his
homeland because they didn't want him to get any of his father's
inheritance. Soon after this, the Ammonites attacked Gilead. His
half-brothers sent for him to come back because they needed him
to help them fight the Ammonites. They told Jephthah that they
would make him commander over the army if he came back to
help them. He accepted their offer and he was the commander
over his brothers. In Judges 11:30-31 (NLT), he made a vow to
the Lord. He said, *If you give me victory over the Ammonites, I*

will give to the Lord whatsoever come out of my house and meet me when I return in triumph. I will sacrifice it as a burnt offering. In Judges 11:32, Jephthah led his army against the Ammonites and the Lord gave him victory. When he returned home to Mizpah, his daughter came out to meet him, playing tambourines and dancing for joy. She was his one and only child. When he saw her, he tore his clothes in anguish. He said, *"Oh my daughter,"* he cried out, *"you have completely destroyed me, you've brought disaster on me, for I have made a vow to the Lord."*

His daughter replied, *You must do to me what you vowed, for the Lord has given you great victory over your enemies, the Ammonites. But first let me do this one thing; let me go up and roam in the hills and weep with my friends for two months, because I will die a virgin* (see Judges 11:37). In Judges 11:39, she returned home and her father kept the vow that he made; she died a virgin. He sacrificed his only seed as a burnt offering to the Lord. He truly understood what it meant to keep his promise to the Lord, even if it meant great and extreme sacrifice. This is a great example of krazy faith.

Galatians 6:7 says, *Be not deceived; God is not mocked: for whatsoever a man soweth, that shall he also reap.* If the seed we sow is planted in good ground, it will produce the harvest of our wildest dreams. 2 Corinthians 9:7-8 (NLT) says, *And we must each decide in the heart how much to give. And, don't give reluctantly or in response to pressure. "For God loves a person who gives cheerfully." Moreover, God will generously provide all you need. Then you will always have everything you need and plenty left over to share with others.*

When it was time for my family and me to transition from the military and decide where we wanted to live, it was vital to listen for and follow the voice of God. God closed the door and my husband was processed out of the military against his desire. However, since he had been laid off from the military, they had to give him severance pay based on his years of service. Both of us were unemployed because we were expecting to transition overseas to our next tour of duty. Instead, my husband was discharged. We had no idea what the next step was going to be. He applied for unemployment, but he was denied because of his severance pay. My family and I lived off the money that my husband received after getting out of the military. But, I believe we lived off nothing but the grace of God. Our rent at that time was $1575. That didn't include monthly utilities. Both of us sought employment daily. My husband had several leads, but no one called to offer him a job.

One day, the Trinity Broadcasting Network, one of the oldest and largest broadcast ministry networks in the world, had their Annual Spring Praise Marathon to raise money. I believe it was our day for a miracle. While watching the marathon, the speaker brought forth a word that spoke directly to our situation.

Dr. Mike Murdock, televangelist and pastor of The Wisdom Center in Louisiana, gave his personal testimony of sowing and reaping and, in the end, being blessed by God because of his obedience.

At the end of his message, he prayed and called for a seed offering. I felt God pressing on my heart to give. I felt a tugging in my spirit to sow a seed. My husband was in the bedroom at that time, so I screamed his name aloud to get his attention. He walked out of the bedroom very quickly. I told him what the Lord laid on my heart and that the seed had to be our best. The first thing that came out of his mouth was, "How much?" He didn't question why we had to give it, nor did he ask me if I was certain or sure. I checked our bank account online. There was only seven hundred dollars left in the bank. That was what we had left to live on.

But even with what seemed to be so little, I felt led to sow five hundred dollars. My husband agreed, but suggested that we pray about it first. We held hands and prayed. I felt my legs shaking out of control and my heart was beating fast. Still, we asked God to move on our family's behalf. I called God's word back to Him. I prayed, "God, you said in Matthew 18:19, if two of us touch and agree concerning anything, it shall be done. My husband and I need a job now, in the name of Jesus. Amen." We thanked God in advance for providing us with employment. We agreed that God's word was true. I called TBN's prayer line and announced that my husband and I were sowing a seed of five hundred dollars.

I hung up the phone and I started worshipping and praising God. I shouted unto the God who is able to do exceedingly, abundantly, above all I can even think. I gave God praise and glory in advance. Pastor Mike Murdock came back after the song was over and he prayed and blessed the offering. I worshipped again, like I was about to lose my mind. I opened my mouth and I declared harvest to come in the name of Jesus! I danced and worshipped God until I felt sweat dripping down my face. I thanked God again in advance for victory. I knew that God had heard our prayers. 1 John 5:14-15 (NLT) says, *And we have confidence that he hears us whenever we ask for anything that pleases him. And since we know he hears us when we make our requests, we also know that he will give us what we ask for.* I knew that it was God's will that my husband and I find employment. We knew that God had our best interest at heart. He promised that He would supply our every need according to His riches in glory by Christ Jesus (see Philippians 4:19)!

God came through that very same hour. When the song was over and the music stopped playing, my telephone rang at that same minute. When I looked at the telephone, I knew it was from a government entity because I recognized the number. I started screaming at the top of my voice. With tears in my eyes, I calmly answered the phone. I was expecting God to perform a miracle, but I didn't know He would provide a sudden miracle, without any delay. I couldn't help but to give God thanks and praise for His goodness before picking up the receiver. The call was for my husband. He came to the phone immediately.

I could hear the person on the phone tell him, "Yes, your tests came back great, and I would like to set up a day for you to come in and get fitted for your uniform because I would like you to start sometime this week." You can only imagine the sound of praise and worship coming out of our apartment. After my husband hung up the phone, we knew that a miracle had taken place. We praised God as if we had lost our minds. I had read many stories in the bible where God showed up immediately or suddenly, but I had never experienced it for myself until that day. It was priceless. God's presence was felt all through that apartment that day. We sowed into the gospel of Jesus Christ and God blessed our faithfulness. God kept His word because of our obedience. Believers should love to give because the word of God says it is better to give than to receive. Sowing and reaping is a kingdom principle. When we sow into the kingdom, our seed does not die; it multiplies. It is the way God increases and meets our needs. We believed what God had promised and because God won't go back on His word, my husband and I received the harvest.

The widow of Zarephath in 1 Kings 17:10-16 understood the value of a seed. This story is also a great example of genuine faith and sowing and reaping. The widow of Zarephath was in possession of her last bit of hope and provision; still she sowed. Because she sowed in faith, she received much more in return. God told Elijah the prophet to go and live in the city of Zarephath. He had already instructed a widow to feed him there. Elijah did according to what God commanded him to do. He went and asked the widow for something to eat.

The woman, however, responded reluctantly, saying she didn't have much to spare at all. In fact, what she had was only enough for the very last meal for herself and her son. Elijah told the widow not to worry about a thing, but to go ahead and first make a small biscuit for him to eat. After that, she could go ahead and make a meal from what would be left for her and her son. He told the woman her jar of flour would not run out and the bottle of oil would not become empty. She stepped out on faith and did exactly what Elijah told her to do. Just like Elijah spoke, because this widow gave her last, her jar with food did not run out and the bottle of oil never became empty. God multiplies what seems like little or not enough. Had this woman not been obedient, she would have not seen the increase. She planted an obedient seed and God brought forth a miracle through Elijah, His prophet. The word of God tells us that when we obey God's prophets, we will prosper (see Chronicles 20:20).

Malachi 3:10 (MSG) says, *Test me in this and see if I don't open up heaven itself and pour out blessings beyond your wildest dreams.* This is the only place in the bible where God calls on the believer to test Him. He wants His children to test Him in our giving. Our God is faithful to His word. Just like this woman, my husband and I were obedient to the voice of God and we reaped a harvest. That very same week, my husband started his new job.

When we took a step of faith, believing God would make provision for us, we too saw miracles, signs and wonders in our lives. Our faith grew.

If you are going through a financial situation right now, please know that God is no respecter of persons. If He showed up for me, He is well able to show up for you, too. Two very important principles for your financial breakthrough are paying your tithes and giving. Adopt an attitude of giving. It will unlock doors that man can't close. If you don't give, then it won't be given to you. Don't look at how much you have because you will never give. The key for your financial breakthrough is giving. Always pray about your situation. When you pray, believe and receive that it is yours. Praise God in advance for what He has already done. Do not respond to what you see in the natural. Speak the word of God over your situation and keep your mind and heart clear of unbelief. When the devil comes in, trying to tell you God won't come through, tell him he is the father of lies and the truth is not in him. Speak, declare and decree God's promises over your situation. Only then will manifestation take place. God loves you. You are fearfully and wonderfully made by Him and He has already given you the best through Jesus Christ. He is a promise keeper. He will never go back on his word. Accept what He has already done by faith.

Psalm 37:23 says *the steps of a good man are ordered by the Lord*! Every day is a new opportunity to take small steps in faith, giving God the opportunity to have His way in our lives. He desires not greatness, but usefulness. When we take small steps in faith, God's glory can be seen. Every situation is an opportunity for miracles, signs and wonders. He is not looking for someone who is great; He is looking for someone whom He can use, someone who serves Him with their whole heart. No word in any language is enough to describe who God is. His ways are indescribable. God moves in my life in those times when I relinquish and totally surrender to His will. He will not move on our behalf when we don't release our situations to Him. God wants to show Himself strong in every situation, and He wants His glory to be evident.

Over fourteen years ago, I gave my heart totally to God. That was the first time I was introduced to tithes and offerings, sowing and reaping. I was always a giver, but I never knew how to produce a harvest. I was the type of believer that was mentioned in Matthew. I cast my seed in gravel. I heard the good news, and instantly responded with enthusiasm. But, there was no soil of character. When the emotions wore off and some difficulty arose, there was nothing to show for it. My husband

and I lived like this for many years, not knowing how to nurture and water our seeds.

I was in church on a Wednesday night when breakthrough came and God freed me. He gave me a revelation of what was happening to my seed. The bible says faith comes by hearing the word of God. The more we hear God's word, the more we grow in our faith. That Wednesday night, my faith grew a bit more thanks to a sermon preached by Pastor Dwayne Brewington of Victory Christian International. I felt free like a bird. It was as if a light switched on in my spirit. That was the very first time that I heard a message on faith of that caliber. He talked about receiving the minute that you plant, speaking to, and calling back your harvest. This was the part I was missing. I often planted and wondered why harvest never came. The pastor then spoke about walking in expectancy to receive from God. –He gave this example. Pretend someone was coming to your house for dinner and they told you they were on their way. One hour passed and they didn't show up. You started looking out of the window, watching eagerly in anticipation that they would show up. Your doorbell rings, you run to the door, open it and find that it's someone else instead of the person you were expecting. You turn around and run back upstairs because you thought you heard the phone, but you were only hearing things. Five minutes later, the doorbell rings again and finally, it is the friend you were originally expecting.

This is the same way we should behave when we plant a seed or when we pray. We target our seed to receive a specific harvest. We declare and decree what the word of God says about our seed. Then, we pray over our seed. We don't only sow money as seed. We can sow God's word. How we treat other people is another way that we sow. I encourage believers to serve and love people because –God *is* love and He serves with humility.

After hearing this message, I was determined to put it into practice. I was determined to win over worrying and doubting, which often caused my seed to die. I guarded my seed by not allowing my flesh to speak negatively or doubt. I study God's word often so I know what God says about what I am praying for.

When worry and doubtful thoughts appear, I shut them down with the word. When we plant a seed, the devil comes in and tempts us by placing thoughts in our minds to try to make us start doubt the capability of our Savior. I was determined to cast down every imagination that was trying to exalt itself against the word of God. I was determined to bring every thought under the obedience of God's word as written in 2 Corinthians 10:5. We have to keep our spiritual eyes open at all times because the devil will try to tempt us. After we have guarded our seed, we walk in thanksgiving and expectancy to receive a harvest.

Even Hannah understood the impact of a seed in I Samuel 1. Hannah had no children, but Elkanah, her husband, had another wife who was able to bear children. Her rival wife, who never let her forget that God had not given her children, taunted Hannah. Every time Hannah went to the sanctuary of God, she was taunted. Hannah was reduced to tears and had no appetite. But she knew the power of a seed. She made a vow to God. 1 Samuel 1:11 (NLT) says, *O Lord of Heaven's Armies, if you will look upon my sorrow and answer my prayer and give me a son, then I will give him back to you. He will be yours for his entire lifetime, and as a sign that he had been dedicated to the Lord, his hair will never be cut.* Hannah understood the importance of a seed. She was without child, and she used her faith in prayer to God. She believed the more-than-enough God to come through and give her a miracle. She stepped out on faith by planting a seed and in the end, it produced a harvest. Hannah knew the God that she served, and she knew she could depend on that friend that sticks closer than a brother (see Proverb 18:24.). She knew by leaning on the everlasting arms of Jesus, she would be rescued and would become the mother of a generation to come. She knew her Heavenly Daddy would intervene and turn her mourning into dancing.

Hannah's vow was a serious one because Ecclesiastes 5:4 tells us that when you make a promise to God, don't delay in following through. God takes no pleasure in fools. We are told to keep all promises we make with Him because it is better to say nothing than to make a promise and not keep it. Ecclesiastes 5:6 tells us to not let our mouths make us sin. God was well pleased with Hannah. She made a vow and she kept her promise. Hannah gave birth to a son, Samuel. 1 Samuel 1:24-28 tells us that when Samuel was weaned, Hannah took him to the temple of the Lord and told Eli that she had made a vow to God that if He gave her a child, she would give him back to the Lord. She promised he would belong to the Lord his whole life. This was an incredible woman of faith. She gave Samuel as a seed unto the Lord, and God heard the cry of this afflicted woman. Not only did He bless her with one more child, God blessed her with seven more children. The number seven is the number of completion and eight is the number of new beginnings (see Genesis 1). Hannah's days of barrenness were over. Not only did God complete what He started, but He blessed this woman of faith with new beginnings. Hannah sowed a seed in faith and God blessed her with many. God put Hannah's enemy to shame.

Each time I read this story, I feel the pain and shame that Hannah must have felt, especially when Peninah tormented her. After more than a decade of marriage, my husband and I were still waiting to get pregnant. We fasted, prayed and cried for a number of years, with no results.

I had it all planned out. By the time my son reached the age of five, we would have another child. The first years of marriage were the hardest because people formed their own conclusions about why we didn't have children. The pain, the shame and the torment were unbearable. The Peninah in my life kept tormenting me. God blessed them with many children, but they tormented me for not having children with my husband. The embarrassment of not being able to give my husband something that was so sacred was difficult. I thought it was so easy to solve. I thought all I had to do was have sex with my husband and that would solve everything. People insisted that I was thinking about it too much. All I needed to do was to live and it would just happen naturally. But, that didn't work at all.

I cried and I cried some more. Still, God said nothing. I had a two-year season of weeping. Every month when my menstrual cycle appeared, matters grew worse. Family members escalated the gossip about my husband. Oh, that hurt me the most. Every time I went around certain people, the first thing they asked was, "You are not pregnant yet?" One person even asked, "Wow! How many years is it now? And you guys are not pregnant yet?" Then she would add, "I know fully who has the problem. It's him; it's not you because you already have a child." Every time she said that, I prayed and cried out, "Lord, hear the affliction of your people!" My husband is an incredible man of faith. To hear someone talk about him like that could not be put into words. The shame, the torment and the embarrassment lasted for many years.

I went through a period of blaming myself, looking at my past sins. Romans 8:1-2 tells us, *So now there is no condemnation for those who belong to Christ Jesus. And because you belong to him, the power of the life giving spirit has freed you from that powerful of sin that leads to death.* Who wouldn't want to serve a God like this? He freed me from my past. I no longer believed the devil's lies anymore. I was free of my past sins because the Son of God had set me free (see John 8:36). So I can relate to how Hannah felt; she was less than sufficient. In spite of it all, we still stood in faith, knowing that God is able.

Through my years of waiting, the Lord brought two different women to me that needed encouragement in their time of waiting. I thought God was tormenting me, though. The first woman crossed my path while I was living in Italy. My husband was stationed there for two years. I believe God took me there just for this young lady. She had been trying to have a child for about four years after suffering a miscarriage. It affected her severely and she was slipping into depression. I prayed and encouraged her for about two years, while still yet trying to find the strength to encourage myself.

Two years later, we both moved to different places. I kept in touch with her, and one day she called me so very excited. She was pregnant! While I was happy for her, sadness came over me and I wept like a small child. The pain I felt was still present. My situation had not been resolved. I felt as though God had forgotten about me. I questioned God. I asked Him why He would place me in a situation like that. Then, I slipped into a time of sadness yet again.

God then moved us from Italy to Maryland. The move was all in the plan of God, because we originally wanted to move to Japan. Instead, we moved into an apartment complex in Germantown, Maryland. Little did I know, I was moving next door to a young woman who also had a miscarriage and was having a difficult time getting pregnant. When I found out that I was moving next door to someone God wanted me to encourage, I looked up to Heaven and said, "Oh no God, not again." When this young lady shared her situation with me, I thought God was tormenting me yet again.

As she shared what she was going through, I knew without any doubt that she was greatly affected by her situation. I started inviting her over to our home for dinner just to encourage her. I assured her that God had not forgotten her. She cried. I consoled her. Most of the time, she left feeling encouraged. Soon after we met, she also became pregnant. I was very happy for her because I knew that God had answered my prayers. I still questioned God, but the pain, on that occasion, wasn't as bad as before. I still felt as though God had forgotten all about me. The pain I felt inside was deep, but I learned that if I helped those who were going through what I was going through, the pain got lighter. I smiled to cover up the way I truly felt. As the years went by, I accepted my condition as God's will. I accepted the pain as part of life. I came to find out that God had a purpose for what seemed like barrenness in my life.

Even in my teenage years, I saw myself having my own baby in my arms. I remember even playing dollhouse, wishing the doll would come alive. My mother told me that when she was a teenager, she asked God for five children, but she never asked Him for a husband with those five children. My mother did have five children out of wedlock. She did eventually get married. I didn't expect the same things that happened to my mom to happen to me, but what I held in my imagination soon led to my reality. I became pregnant right out of high school. Never did I think I would be pregnant and alone. This was the first time I recognized how much we have the power to bring things to life that are in our imagination.

Sharing my pregnancy with my mother wasn't easy at all. Telling a Guyanese parent that you were pregnant and not married meant the risk of a beat down or even peppering. Peppering, according to what I have heard, is when parents hold a young lady down and place hot pepper into her private parts. I believe the whole practice was really just a threat, part of my culture's belief of putting fear into a teenager. When a young lady shows interest in the opposite sex, my culture calls her hot. Showing interest in the opposite sex does not mean a young lady is being promiscuous. A great number of our young people are being brought up in single-family households, which may have a great effect on their upbringing. I was brought up in a partially fatherless home and I always felt as though there was something missing. I needed to be loved. My stepfather lived with us for a short time and it was during that time that I felt secure as a teen. A father or father figure in a home is so important. I believe the church is a place of refuge. The church is a place where young people should be able to come and hear the word, and receive love unconditionally. It is not a place where they should be looked down upon because they become teenaged parents. The love of God covers a multitude of sin. I am not saying dust it under the rug. But, speak the truth in love when God leads and love them like crazy. This is how we will change generations to come.

I believe my early life was all for the glory and honor of God. I can share what I experienced with young people. Having a baby out of wedlock wasn't easy at all. Today, it is still a struggle, but God has brought me a mighty long way.

I have also learned that we can invite torment and taunting into our lives when we miss the fact that we are harboring ill emotions in the crevices of our hearts. My husband and I started raising my son together when he was four years old. When I wrote this book, he was just a couple of years shy of being a legal adult. My son's biological father was in and out of his life. In fact, when I got married, I was in the process of trying to find him so that I could petition him for child support. My incredible husband told me to stop trying because he was going to take full responsibility for him as his son.

Over the years, my son saw his biological father occasionally. Without even realizing it, I had carried hurt and distrust from the time my son was a baby. As my son got older and would mention his father's name, my heart would pump really fast. I recalled all the bad events that took place in our relationship. Because of this, and the lack of support, I didn't want to hear his name. This went on for sixteen years. I did not realize that what I was carrying was having an emotional effect on my son. He kept his feelings about his biological dad locked deep inside. Because I did not trust his father with him, their time together was limited. As my son got older, I let go a little, but just enough to *say* that my son spent time with him. Even still, my husband and I did our best to teach him how to love his dad. Deep down inside, my son wanted more.

The summer of 2013, my husband and I went through the test of our lives. We decided to let my son be a part of the decision-making. We consulted him when it came to how long he wanted to spend at his biological dad's house. During this summer of testing, he told us he only wanted to spend two weeks with him. Never did we imagine that when it was time to come back home that his dad would call to inform us that my son wasn't coming back to live with us. He had apparently made a decision to live with his father.

Well, of course, I didn't believe anything my son's father was saying because I wanted to hear it directly from my son's mouth. I never imagined hearing these words, "Mommy, I am not coming back. I want to stay here with my dad." My heart broke in a thousand pieces. It was a feeling that I couldn't describe in words. I found out the whole matter was planned by my son and his dad before he was even picked up for his summer trip. My heart was crushed.

Even worse, my son began to treat my husband, who had raised him for so many years, as if he didn't know him. He treated him as if he was a complete stranger. He refused to talk to him on the phone and every time my son called, he acted as if my husband wasn't even there. The night we got that dreaded call, I only got about three hours of sleep. To be honest, I felt a little of what Jesus must have felt when His own people rejected Him. It hurt like crazy. I could not stop crying. I even felt the pain and disappointment my husband was feeling. But God!

I woke up the following morning for my 5:30 a.m. prayer and I lifted my hands in faith. I could hardly talk to God. I was completely broken. I worshipped God with the few words I could speak and with tears running down my face. As the days went on, it became more difficult because my son continued to plead with me to let him stay with his father. I asked God what

His desire was. In my spirit, I knew God's will was for him to come home, but my flesh felt like letting him go so he could see the grass was not greener on the other side. I held on to my son in prayer as I allowed the Holy Spirit to lead me.

Something great happened out of this terrible experience. First, my son's father and I began having normal conversations for the first time in sixteen years. I realized the image of him that I was holding on to was not correct at all. I realized that I was holding onto un-forgiveness. This really surprised me because I thought I had dealt with my emotions when I received Christ as my personal Savior. I thought I had let go of past hurts. When we started talking and actually listening to each other, I discovered that we wanted the same things for our son. He wanted my son to have a life he never had and so did I. I felt as though a load had been lifted off of me. I felt as though he was now part of the team of raising my son.

I thanked God for the trial because it showed me what was in my heart. I believe God healed me of un-forgiveness through this whole ordeal. One morning after prayer, following the leading of the Holy Spirit, I called him and told him that I forgave every past and present hurt he had inflicted on me. It was pure quietness on his end. I knew he was very surprised because I was reaching out to him with the love of God. I told him I loved him with the love of God. When I hung up the phone, I felt as though I had an out-of-body experience. I knew that the spirit of the Lord had taken over and in all that had happened, God's glory was revealed.

From that day, I was totally free from the pain of my past. About three weeks later, my son came home and I was tested again on forgiveness. In a very heated discussion I was having with my son's father, I brought up the past. But the convicting power of the Holy Spirit fell on me. I immediately shifted my conversation to the present. Then, I knew God had set me free of the bondage of un-forgiveness and I knew without a shadow of doubt, a seed of forgiveness and God's love was planted in his heart.

God loves us and forgives us of our past. So, why can't we forgive others? You too can accept what Jesus did over 2,000 years ago. All you have to do is accept Him as your personal Savior and He'll take your sins, throw them in the sea of forgetfulness, and remember them no more. He will give you joy, peace, love, patience, kindness, goodness, faithfulness, gentleness, long-suffering, and self-control, all of which are free.

Over sixteen years ago, through all of my pain and distress, I knew I had prayer warriors praying for me. My grandmother, a woman of faith, was praying that God would save me. She never stopped praying because she knew Heaven would answer. When I was little, she sowed the word of God into my siblings and me. But I strayed. I had a son out of wedlock. I came to Christ broken and my heart needed fixing badly. Through all of my pain and hang-ups, I knew God would turn it all around for the good. I remember one day, lying flat on the floor and the Holy Spirit reassured me that my son was born into the world for purpose. He will use my son to bring greater glory to Himself.

When I got saved, I gave myself completely to God. I asked Him to help me keep myself pure for my husband. I made a vow to commit myself totally to God. After making that vow, a counterfeit came. I knew the devil had heard my vow. I met someone and the first thing I did was asked him if he was saved. He said he went to church occasionally. Therefore, I quickly told him there was no way we could see each other. He kept trying to buy me with gifts and favors, but I paid him no mind and eventually he stopped calling. Two years passed and God gave me the strength to keep my promise to Him. God blessed me with an incredible man of faith, Robert. He is a Godsend. After more than a decade together, he still wants to be by my side. Every time I am feeling down, he lifts me up with the word of God. He prays for me and with me. He accepted our children as his own. His heart is big with love for his family and everyone around him.

Chapter 6
Blind Faith

In Mark 8:22-26, we find the story of Jesus healing a blind man. When Jesus arrived in Bethesda, a blind man was brought before him. Jesus took the blind man by the hand and led him out of the village. Then Jesus spit on the man's eyes, laid his hands on them, and asked him, "Can you see anything now?" The man looked around and responded, "Yes. I see people, but I can't see them very clearly." Jesus placed his hands on the man's eyes again, and his sight was completely restored. He could see everything clearly. This story of Jesus healing the blind man reminds me of believers before coming to Christ. We all are blind in sin. Yet when we come to know Christ as our personal Savior, Jesus uncovers our eyes and unlocks our hearts so that we too can see clearly. Jesus performed this miracle and then led the healed man out of the village. Obviously, that wasn't the place Jesus wanted to perform that miracle. Jesus even told the blind man not to go back into the village. The thing that empowers me in this story is Jesus leading the blind man out of the city.

Not only can I relate to Jesus healing my sight, but I can also relate to how the once-blind man must have felt as Jesus led him out of the city. There was a season in my life when I felt as though I was without my sight. During that time, in every minute, I felt as though Jesus was holding my hands, leading and ordering my every step. I had to walk through a season of blindness. This kind of faith is not easy at all, even though we are directed to live our lives from minute to minute because tomorrow is not promised to any man. In this season, my husband and I had no idea where we were going to live, what we were going to eat or where we were going to work. It was no joke. There was no family member close by to extend us a bed for a night or two. We had to walk through this season one step at a time and we had to use pure faith. We were in a situation where the only option was to trust God.

My husband came out of the military unexpectedly. One day, he was awaiting word on his next duty station. By the next day, he was transitioning out of the military. Just like in our other military moves, I packed our life into boxes, gave up the apartment we were living in and waited to be moved. My husband was stationed in Bahrain at that time. He phoned home and simply said, "Baby, I am getting out of the military." Well, with no plan, tough days were ahead. I turned my plate over, prayed and cried out to the Lord. God said nothing. God knew I was comfortable being a military spouse, so He decided to take me out of my comfort zone. My husband made his way back home, unsure of his next move. In fact, the new tenant was scheduled to move in a week after he arrived home. We were three days away from needing to vacate the apartment, and still God said nothing.

One day before we had to move, I woke up determined to search until I found where God was leading. I walked into my complex rental office and first asked for an extension. The secretary looked me right in the face and said, "Mama, there is no way possible. You have to move out in two days."

Well, every hour, every minute was difficult because I knew we needed to find somewhere to live really fast. I knew there was no way on earth that God would want my family to be homeless. Every morning after that day, my husband and I spent days looking for somewhere to call home. This was extremely difficult because every place we visited asked about employment. Neither one of us was working at that time. I felt completely blind. I had no idea where to go or what to do. However, I knew God was leading us the same way He led that blind man out of the village. The devil placed fear into our spirits about being homeless. My husband and I took long walks around the neighborhood, holding hands and praying, asking God for direction. I woke up one morning and the Holy Spirit told me to go back to the rental office, but to inquire about a two-bedroom apartment. When I walked into the rental office, I began thanking God in advance for His favor. God's favor was evident! They did have a smaller apartment that was move-in ready. We were approved on the spot. They didn't ask about income because we already had good standing with paying our rent. I remember moving into that small two-bedroom apartment, thanking God for the roof over our heads. Sometimes, we take the small things for granted. I thanked God for bringing us through a very scary and difficult season.

If you are going through a difficult season, know that God is well able to do exceedingly, abundantly, above all that you can even ask or think. He will lead you the same way that He led that blind man. Take your hands off of the situation. If you are trying to solve your situation yourself, God can't move. Get rid of unbelief. When you mix faith with doubt and worry, your harvest will be delayed or cancelled. Destroy worry and doubt by standing on the promises of God and choose to believe God's word today.

When we moved into our two-bedroom apartment, we had to rent a storage unit because all of our stuff could not fit. We were still thankful because God made a way for us. One day, my mother called me and asked me if my nephew could come live with us because he was getting into a lot of trouble in school. He was suspended within the first two weeks of the new school year. In addition, my brother had a very busy schedule and it was hard for my nephew to compete his homework assignments on his own after school. My husband and I prayed and asked God for direction before agreeing. We opened our tiny apartment to my nephew. Even though it was already too small for us, we took a leap of faith because we loved him. We ended up finding a sofa bed for my nephew to sleep on. It was tough to adjust to this crowded apartment, but we were able to get by. Meanwhile, my husband and I started believing God for a house. Of course, we had no money for a down payment, but we believed our faith was enough.

We believed that God would supply our every need according to His riches in glory (Philippians 4:19). We believed that was good enough. It wasn't long before we found a brand-new house that was in the process of being built. When we saw the model and the size, it was perfect for our family. Neither one of us had a suitable job, but that didn't disqualify us from receiving a miracle from God. I was working a seasonal position at JC Penney, making $8.50 an hour. My husband had been offered a job, but he hadn't started it yet. We went into the model home and we loved it. We filled out the application by faith. We told the sales representative that my husband was about to start his new job in about a week, and the sales representative based our income according to what was expected. My husband's soon-to-be-supervisor informed him he would be averaging sixty hours a week. Based on that, we were pre-approved for our brand-new home on the spot. That same day, the sales representative, David, told us we needed three thousand, five hundred dollars as a down payment to secure the home.

There was no way on earth that was going to happen without God. We made our way home and decided to claim that new house as ours. We prayed, thanking God in advance for first blessing us with favor and grace. The salesman then told us we could pay him the down payment in installments immediately. We thanked God in advance for providing the money. A week later, God made a way for us to give them the first seven hundred dollars. Even though God was making a way, the enemy was still fighting against the plan of God. Things took a turn for the worse. My husband did start working as planned, but the hours promised were not fulfilled. In addition, my job at JC Penney ended.

I knew God hadn't brought us that far to leave us. Fear crept in, but I knew fear hadn't come from God. I knew it was the trick of the enemy. The salesman called us every day because he wanted us to complete the deposit. The bank wanted to see our most recent pay stubs. We avoided answering the phone for a while because we simply didn't know what to say. We knew we needed to speak to God to ask for direction. When I spoke to David, I advised him about my husband's decreased hours and my job situation. The bank also told us because of the decreased hours and loss of job, we needed twenty thousand dollars more income in order to qualify for a mortgage. We prayed and left it in the hands of God.

While I was looking for a job, I prayed and asked God to open the door. Meanwhile, David kept calling, asking about the balance of the down payment. Still, he made it clear that he would wait and hold the house until I found a job. We kept thanking God in advance for making a way. I praised Him for His unending favor in my life because clearly, He was speaking to the salesman's heart. Meanwhile, when doubt crept in, I spoke the word. My family and I took several trips to our new house. We parked our vehicle in front of our new home and spoke the word over it. We would say, "This home is ours and we claim it in the name of Jesus!" We spoke about it as if we already had it. Whenever we passed the exit on the interstate, we would say, "Pretty soon, we will be taking this exit to go home." We even started packing our stuff into boxes. We also told our storage company we were moving out soon. We did this for about two months while our house was being built. We sealed every prayer by thanking God for what He had already done.

Not before long, I was called for a job interview. I was so excited to tell David I was closer to finding a job. I was offered a position, which guaranteed twenty to thirty hours a week. Not only did I find employment, but God also made a way for us to pay our next installment. We received more favor when the salesman told us we could bring the balance with us to closing.

When we're facing difficult times, we try to solve it on our own. But God doesn't need us. He is well capable of handling every situation. He just wants us to trust, depend and totally commit ourselves to Him.

After working for about six weeks, we were faced with another obstacle. I received a call from the bank saying that I needed more hours in order for us to qualify for the house. I needed to be in a full-time position instead of part-time. I didn't know what to do, but pray for direction again. I knew I had to ask for increased hours, but my director wasn't an easy person to talk to. Most of the employees were afraid of her. Still, my husband and I prayed and agreed in the name of Jesus that God would speak to her heart. I knew without a shadow of a doubt that God heard us.

Matthew 17:20 (NLT) says, *I tell you the truth, if you have faith even as small as a mustard seed, you can say to this mountain, 'move from here to there,' and it will move. Nothing will be impossible.* That verse was active in my spirit the morning as I drove to work, expecting to receive additional work hours. In fact, I gave God praise and thanks in advance, again, for His favor. I walked into the building and headed straight into my director's office. My legs were shaking of control. I said, "Good morning. Can I have a word with you please?"

Then she said, "I was just about to call you into my office this morning." She asked what I wanted. I told her I was in the process of buying a home and the bank advised me that I needed to work full time in order to qualify for the mortgage.

She looked at me and asked, "Were you praying? Do you believe in God?" She was Muslim, and I really didn't understand why she was asking. I looked at her puzzled as she slid a piece of paper on her desk in front of her toward me. She said, "The reason I was about to call you into my office is because I was going to offer you a full-time position, which guaranteed forty hours a week."

Before saying anything, I needed to process what she had just said. Then I said, "Are you saying you had already filled out this application and was about to call me to let me know that you're giving me a full-time position?"

She responded, "Yes." She asked me to sign my name on the line stating that I accepted the position. I signed, with my hands shaking, in awe of another of God's miracles. I left her office, speechless. God had showed up again. Even before I stepped into that building, He had already worked it out. Hallelujah! God is good!

God loves us with an everlasting love (see Jeremiah 31:3). He is always willing to give us His best if we just trust, lean and depend on Him. All we need is a little faith. Our faith size just needs to be as large as a mustard seed. A mustard seed is very tiny. So our faith doesn't need to be big at all. 2 Corinthians 9:8 says, *God is able to make all grace abound towards you; that ye, always having all sufficiency in all things.*

This was not the end of the miracle concerning our brand new home. Our sales representative told us we needed to bring one thousand dollars with us to closing, which was the balance of the down payment. The morning of the closing, I was so excited because this was my first home. We used our faith and God had come through. At the closing, we signed our life away on what seemed like ten thousand pieces of papers. When all of it was finished, the woman stood up, shook our hands, and gave us the keys to our new home. Then, I whispered in my husband's ear, "Baby, how come she didn't ask us for the money? David told us to bring this check with us at closing, didn't he?" My husband nodded his head in confirmation. I decided to ask, "Excuse me, ma'am. David told us to bring this check with us at closing. Are you going to collect it?"

She asked, "What check are you talking about?" Then she said, "Hold on one minute, let me check the file again." She flipped through the pile of paperwork that was sitting in front of her and then said, "No, there is no record of money that needs to be collected." She continued, "Oh sorry, I forgot to tell you. You get to live mortgage-free for the first month."

I yelled, "What?" I was in a state of shock and awe.

She responded, "There is no need to pay your mortgage because it is not due until the following month."

I couldn't believe we had gone to closing and instead of paying them money, they ended up giving us a month free on our mortgage.

The blessing of God will overtake you for sure. The blessing of the Lord makes us rich, and adds no sorrow with it (see Proverbs 10:22). We ran out of that building with our check, thanking God for His goodness toward us. We praised and worshipped God like we were crazy. Deuteronomy 28:2 talks about God's blessings overtaking us. In this season, I felt overwhelmed by the love of God.

In addition, something else wonderful happened after we had been in our new home only a couple of months. I was having a conversation with a co-worker about how much I believed God for an unexpected check. I was overwhelmed with lingering bills. The same day that I had that conversation with my co-worker, I came home and there was a check in my mailbox from my mortgage company for nine hundred dollars. The accompanying letter said it was a refund for an overcharge. What a mighty God we serve! Angels bow before Him, Heaven and earth adore Him. What a mighty God we serve! If I had ten thousand tongues, I still would not know how to praise Him enough. He is just that good to me. I couldn't stop screaming and praising God. It was a mere desire that I had, but I had not prayed or asked God. He blessed us because He is a faithful God. Psalm 37: 4 says, *Delight thyself also in the Lord; and he shall give thee the desires of thine heart.*

Romans 4:16-17 (MSG) says, *The fulfillment of God's promises depend entirely on trusting God and His ways, and then simply embracing Him and what He does. God's promises arrive as pure gifts; that's the only way everyone can be sure to get in on it, those who keep the religious traditions and those who have never heard them. For Abraham is a father of us all. He is not our racial father; He is our father of faith. We call Abraham "father" not because He got God's attention by living like a saint, but because God made something of Abraham when he was nobody. Abraham dared to trust God. When everything was going wrong, Abraham believed anyway; deciding not to live what he couldn't do, but rely on what God said he would do. And the Bible says, and so he was made father of multitude of peoples.*

Romans 4:19-25 (MSG) says, *Abraham didn't focus on his own impotence by saying, "It's hopeless. This 100-year-old body could never father a child." Nor did he survey Sarah's decades of infertility and give up. He didn't tiptoe around God's promise, asking curiously skeptical questions. He plunged into the promise and came up strong, ready for God, sure that God would make good on what He had said. That's why it is said, "Abraham was declared fit for trusting God to set him right." But it is not just Abraham; it's also us! The same thing gets said about us when we embrace and believe the One who brought Jesus to life when conditions were equally hopeless.*

Abraham is an example to all of us. He trusted and believed what God said. A person who put their trust in Christ is like Abraham. They are a child of faith. When we live by faith, we are blessed along with Abraham. Therefore, we are the heirs of our forefather Abraham (see Galatians 3:7-9). My brothers and sisters, God really loves us. He loves us with an incredible love that only the Holy Father can give His children. His love is unending and never failing toward those who fear Him. This is the meaning of true love.

My grandmother experienced this unending, never failing love here on earth before transitioning to Glory. She was an incredible woman of faith. She truly loved and stood on the promises of God. Vioda December was married to George December, my grandfather. He was an alcoholic and she was a prayer warrior. When George December came home drunk as a fish, he cursed and acted out. My grandmother fought in the spirit. She spoke to the demonic forces that were in operation. Then, my grandfather would either leave immediately or go to sleep.

Vioda spent her days fixing George's dinner and have it waiting for him in a glass dish. George often decided that he didn't want it, and he would dispose of it without having any regrets. My grandmother didn't let that stop her. She still fixed his meal nicely every night. How she treated him did not depend on him. She loved her alcoholic husband, even when times were difficult. Her life truly exemplified Christ. She not only raised my brothers, sisters and I, but she raised other family members, too. She believed in prayer, fasting and God's word, which she took very seriously. She got up at four o'clock every morning and met God most of her years here on earth. She believed in miracles, signs and wonders. When things seemed out of whack, she turned her plate over and fasted and prayed until things changed.

When my sister Marcel needed surgery for an abnormal chest condition, my grandmother decided that wasn't going to happen. She prayed and fasted for three days. After consecrating herself, she took my sister back to the doctors, who determined there was no need to have surgery. My grandmother stood firmly on what she believed. She had the kingdom of God living on the inside of her. She not only talked about Jesus to every person that she met, but she demonstrated what she believed by the way she lived.

Her beliefs manifested in answered prayers consistently. I was told that my grandmother's prayers came to pass when my father entered into a relationship he should not have. My dad moved in with a lady, whom he wasn't married to. My grandmother turned her plate over for seven days, seeking resolution in the matter. On the eighth day, my dad came walking out of the lady's home with his bags flung across his shoulders. Not only did she experience miracles because of her prayers, but she also led many people to Christ. It is because of my grandmother's prayers that I am saved today. I can also say God also used my mother to water the seed that my grandmother planted when I was little. I remember during my teenage years, my mother got up early every morning and cried out to God on behalf of her children. He heard their prayers and He gave the increase.

I don't know what situation you might be facing today. But I know prayer works. Even when it looks like it is not working, or things are not changing, they are. Prayer works. My grandmother's prayers were answered. My grandfather, the alcoholic, was saved on his dying bed. Thank you Lord for grace and mercy; he is in Heaven. A perfect stranger led him to the Lord before he took his last breath. Some of my grandmother's answered prayers outlived her. She prayed for one of my cousins to accept Christ before her death, but my cousin did not commit her life to Christ until seven years after my grandmother had passed.

Don't be dismayed. Even though it seems like your prayers are unanswered, the bible says that God sits high and He looks low on His people. Everything you have asked for is already done. Give Him thanks in advance! Keep on praying, keep on believing. It is already done.

God has no more respect for one person than He does for another, nor does God show favoritism (see Romans 2:11). He heard the prayers of this little old woman and because she knew how to touch Heaven, God answered. My grandmother passed away in 2002, but her legacy still lives in us today. She left a legacy of prayers and intercession for generations to come. If you ask most people what kind of legacy they want to leave for their children, they would probably say something tangible. There is nothing wrong with leaving those things, but what if our children lost everything? What would they do then? How would they cope with the loss? Leaving them a legacy of Jesus is the most important of all. They should know how to believe God for the impossible. They should know how to pray and fast until change takes place. They should know how to win souls for Christ because in the end, only what they do for Christ will last. My greatest desire is that my children know how to live a life that is pleasing to the Father. My desire is to teach them how to commit, trust and believe in the word of God.

One morning, before my grandmother passed on to glory, she didn't wake up early for prayer like she normally did. She decided to sleep in. But, none of my cousins wanted to check on her because they thought that she was dead. That is how much she devoted herself to prayer and reading the word of God. While on her dying bed, my grandmother prayed for all of her grandkids, children and everyone around her. Then, she repented for all wrongdoing and she went home to be with the Lord, where there is no more sadness, grief, pain or suffering. I can imagine the angels of God welcoming her. I can imagine how beautiful she looks in her Heavenly body, young and slim. I can imagine her Savior saying, "Welcome home, my good and faithful servant. Welcome home!"

When my grandmother passed away, my husband and I went back to my country for the funeral. We had the chance to meet and later adopt the most beautiful princess, Carisha Nicola. My grandmother was raising her because her mother committed suicide. I had never considered adopting a child, but I believed it was the plan of God. My daughter is the most loving young lady that I have ever met. She instantly bonded to my husband and me. The process of the adoption was not easy at all. We had to fly back and forth from Italy to England, then to Guyana because of various stages of the adoption. We used our faith in God to work miracles for us. God made a way, step by step. When we thought the adoption was nearly complete, I flew from Italy to New York and then to Guyana. When I got to Guyana, I discovered the lawyer we were paying had been sitting on the paperwork, which brought the adoption process to a standstill. I left the adoption office feeling totally defeated. On my way back to my cousin's house, I was sitting beside an angel, a woman of faith, whom I had never met before. She prayed with me and assured me that everything would work out. She said God would come through, and she encouraged me to keep my faith in Him.

I left my country feeling so encouraged. I started preparing myself, as if my daughter had come back with me. I started buying clothes and preparing my home for another person. Hebrews 11:1,6 says, *Now faith is the substance of things hoped for, the evidence of things not seen. But without faith it impossible to please him: for he that cometh to God must believe that he is, and that he is a rewarded of them that diligently seek him.* After that trip, my husband and I prayed constantly. We sought God for His will. A few months later, the adoption was over. I had to once again fly from Italy to New York, and then to my country. God showed up many more times in the process and my daughter was released to come to America. We thanked God for the goodness and favor He bestowed upon us. When we step out on faith, God performs miracles through our lives. When we trust in God's ability and not our own, God's will was accomplished on earth as it is in Heaven.

Chapter 7
No Fear in Faith

2 Timothy 1:7 says, *For God hasn't given us a spirit of fear; but of power, and of love, and a sound mind.* Faith and fear are enemies. Faith comes by hearing the word of God, but fear comes from listening to the devil's lies. When we meditate on the lies of the enemy, fear is present and we cannot experience God. Job was a great man of faith, but he lived in fear. Because he lived in fear, the very things he feared came upon him (see Job 3:25). Fear is a spirit and it doesn't come from God. Job declared his own destiny by allowing fear to creep in and make a home in his heart. Faith and fear cannot live in the same house. Fear can destroy destiny and eventually, destroys us. Once it has found a place in our hearts, our faith cannot operate. The only

remedy that we can use to destroy fear is to speak the word of God directly to fear. We cannot just speak it in our minds. We have to literally open our mouths and declare faith and rebuke fear. Fear torments us and we live a life of defeat and uncertainty because we don't know who we are in Christ. 2 Corinthians 10:5 says we must C*ast down every imaginations and every high thing that exalteth itself against the knowledge of God, and bring into captivity every thought to the obedience of Christ.* Christians must take *all* thoughts that are contrary to the word of God captive.

I had the opportunity to experience this recently. My husband was on long deployment overseas, and my children and I were left alone. The spirit of fear overtook me. For weeks, I walked with fear without even realizing it. I spent most nights jumping out of my sleep, troubled with tormenting thoughts. This went on for a while. I would get up and walk around the house, checking the windows, the doors, the kids' rooms and looking outside several times to make sure no one was trying to break in. It was very time consuming. Consequently, I was exhausted during the day since I was up all night. I believe that the Lord freed me from this when I was watching Creflo Dollar on television as he spoke on fear. He said, "When it comes, we have to speak the word of God over it." He said we shouldn't just declare the word in our minds; we had to actually declare it out of our mouths. I decided to apply what he said. I searched the bible and found 2 Timothy 1:7. I declared it out loud until it got into my spirit. The very next time I woke up in fear, I started declaring the word of God into the atmosphere and directly to the devil. I told the devil that he had tortured me too long and I was serving him notice. Immediately, it disappeared. I slept like a baby for the rest of the night. Of course, I was tested again. When I woke up again in the middle of the night, I repeated that scripture and went back to sleep. That was the last night I woke up in fear.

If you are going through something similar, know that God can free you right now. Every time fear appears, read 2 Timothy 1:7 and declare it to the devil. Then, watch it disappear. Make sure you speak it out loud and clear. Tell that spirit of fear that it has to get out of your life in the name of Jesus. Receive your freedom today, in the name of Jesus!

1 John 4:18 says, *There is no fear in love; but perfect love casteth out fear: because fear has torment. He that feareth is not made perfect in love.* Oh, how I love this verse! If we know that our Father loves us, the word of God says those who believe can enter into rest (see Hebrews 4:3). We can rest in the arms of Jesus, knowing that He will protect and provide for us. If we are not resting in God, fear can creep in and make its way into our hearts. Another instance, fear crept into my home yet again, and I didn't realize it. I believe it crept in when I was watching a report on the local news about gay men being attacked and

beaten. For some reason, this got into my spirit and fear tried to torment me. The fear came about my son Amari, who is not gay. One day, I was sitting around my dinner table and my son stood up and began imitating gay men. While I have nothing against gay men, I totally disagree with the sin. If you are gay or straight, I believe God loves us all the same. We are commanded by Him to love one another, and that is what I teach my children. I shared this example only because I want to show just how real fear is. The only way we can win against it is to speak the word so that spirit can flee from us.

When my son started imitating gay men, fear got louder. A few days later, I was on my way to church and a light switched on in my spirit. I felt as though God had taken the veil from my eyes. I sat there in the front seat of my vehicle, and the Holy Spirit dropped it into my spirit that I was dealing with a spirit of fear concerning my son. I had an "Aha!" moment. My husband was driving. I was in the passenger seat and my teens were in the backseat. Then, I started to speak to the devil aloud. I called him a liar. I told him he was the father of all liars. Then, I told him to stop lying to me about my son being gay. I whipped out 2 Timothy 1:7 on him, and I rebuked him in the name of Jesus. My family looked at me as if I had lost my mind. I really didn't mind looking crazy in front of them because I had to expose the plan of the enemy. He was trying to plant a seed into my heart that was tormenting me.

Believers should expose the enemy's plans and come against him with the word of God. This pleases our Father. At that time, I told my family what was happening. They all looked at me in amazement. They were very surprised by what came out of my mouth. Still, I decreed the word of God. The Holy Spirit spoke to me again and said, "The battlefield is in your mind. The enemy is mostly after our hearts." If he can plant a seed in our hearts, then he has us. What's in our hearts will soon make its way through our mouths. I knew instantly that was the truth from God and once I exposed the devil that Sunday, I was free. It hasn't returned since.

The very first time the devil brings any thoughts to our minds that are contrary to God's word, we must demolish those thoughts with the truth of the word of God. If not, that thought will root itself into our spirits and become a reality. Remember, what Job feared became a reality. To be free from fear, we have to have knowledge of the word of God and know what it says in order to fight the good fight of faith. God has given us His word because He knew we'd need it. He knew that without His word, we would be nothing. Every believer can experience victory in over fear if we know how to fight against the evil one. The word of God is our weapon of mass destruction. Fighting with natural words will only stir up confusion. The evil one is the author of all confusion.

Our fight is not against flesh and blood, but *against principalities, against powers and rulers of the darkness of this world, against spiritual wickedness in high places* (see Ephesians 6:12). But God has given us weapons for spiritual warfare. Ephesians 6:10-12 says, *God is strong and he wants you strong. So take everything The Master has set out for you, well-made weapons made with the best materials. And put them to use so that you will be able to stand up to everything the Devil throws your way. This is no afternoon athletic contest that we'll walk away from and forget about in a couple of hours. This is for keeps, a life-or death- fight to the finish against the Devil and all his angles.* We must be prepared to fight the good fight of faith against the evil one. We must learn how to apply truth with prayer in order to win every time. This fight will last until we go on to be with God or until He comes back for His children. So every believer must be equipped with the word of God if they want victory in every area of their lives. We must know the truth and only then will we be set free. Hebrews 4:12 says, *For the word of God is quick, and powerful, and sharper than any two-edged sword, piercing even to the dividing asunder of soul and spirit.* God's words can tear through the hardest heart. The enemy doesn't stand a chance against it.

Going back to the example of my son, I wasn't aware that spirit of fear had entered through my eyes. My defenses were down and the devil came in and knocked me down. The enemy had fun, showing me images that weren't true. I had gone through this before but I wasn't able to use my weapon because I was not paying attention. In Luke 21:36, the word of God warns us that we must watch and pray always. Believers must always be ready to fight the good fight of faith. When the devil throws us a punch, we must throw him back the word of God. We must stand, having our loins girded about with truth and having on the breastplate of righteousness. In order for faith to work, there must be an absence of fear.

The story of Shadrach, Meshach and Abednego in Daniel 3 is a great example of men who had no fear of being destroyed for refusing to bow down false images. They knew if they didn't bow down to that statue, they would immediately be thrown into the blazing furnace. In Daniel 3:16-18 (MSG), they said to the king, (after he gave them another chance to bow down to the statue): *Your threats mean nothing to us. If you throw us in the fire, the God we serve can rescue us from your roaring furnace and anything else you might cook up, O king. But even if he doesn't, it wouldn't make a bit of difference, O king. We still wouldn't serve your God or worship the gold statue you set up.* These boys are good examples to all of us. Even when we find ourselves at the end of our rope, we can still say, "The God we serve is well able to deliver us." Even when fear comes into our hearts and tries to steal our joy, we can still say the God we serve is well able to deliver us out of the hands of the evil one. These boys had hope and confidence in the one true and living God, Jehovah Jireh, the God who always provides a way of escape. In fact, they even told the king that even if God didn't rescue them, it wouldn't make any difference. They still wouldn't bow down and worship his golden statue. They used their faith to stand strong in the face of idolatry. Their faith had no doubt, worry, fear or unbelief. These three Hebrew boys refused to bow down to the statue and in the end they were thrown into the fiery furnace. But God! He showed up with them in the furnace and rescued them. The word of God says not a hair on their head was burned.

Have you ever been in a situation where you said to God, "God, even if you don't show up, I will still serve you?" Alternatively, "Lord, even if I die, you are still God. Lord even if the cancer takes over, I will still worship you until my dying day." Whatever your *even if* is, the good news is that God has already answered your request. His word will never come back empty. You are the righteousness of God. The work was finished when our Savior rose again on the third day.

Healing is our birthright. Everything we need is already made available to all believers by faith. We are the seed of Abraham and if God showed up for the three Hebrew boys, He will also show up for us. God is faithful, morning by morning, new mercies we see. He loves His children and that is why He comes to our rescue. When we hold fear captive to the word of

God, we live a life of pure faith. Believers should not play with the spirit of fear because it shows we don't have any knowledge about who we are in Christ. If we live fear-free, we can then experience the fullness of our Father's blessing.

Chapter 8
Walking by Faith Toward Harvest

2 Corinthians tells us to walk by faith, not by what we see. Our step towards harvest does not depend on what see, hear, smell or what we feel; it depends on the truth of God's word. Our five senses always contradict our faith. Faith is what brings about harvest. Faith in God will make a demand on what rightfully belongs to us. We are the children of God and we are heirs to the promise together with Jesus Christ. Since we have this birthright, nothing moves God but our faith. Our emotion or our tears do not move Him. He is moved by pure faith. Faith and prayer are what unlock the doors to the impossible.

A couple of months after moving into our new home, we were flooded with bills and the new mortgage payment. We were so overwhelmed with it all. My husband got paid and all we saw was enough to pay the mortgage. We had so many outstanding bills that urgently needed to be paid. In fact, our utilities were in great risk of being terminated. When we finished paying our tithes and offering, we could have very well paid our mortgage, but my husband and I decided that we would step out on faith and pay our utility bills since disconnection was certain. When everything was paid, we were short about $1450, which was needed to make up the mortgage payment. In fact, we had no other paycheck that was coming for another two weeks.

I prayed and asked God to make a way or give us the direction to take. Then one morning, the answer about what to do came to me. I remembered Dr. Creflo Dollar preached a word that changed my life. He said, "If you have a bill that is due and you don't have enough money to pay it, it's a seed." I jumped off my bed, ran downstairs and suggested to my husband that we plant a seed toward our mortgage payment. My husband, an incredible man of faith, said without thinking about it, "Yes, let's do it!" We prayed and then planted ten percent of what was needed. We opened our mouths and declared the word of God over our seed and immediately began walking in expectancy. I checked the mailbox regularly in anticipation of my harvest. Every day, I thanked God for making a way in advance. My husband asked me every day if the blessing had come yet. I kept replying that it hadn't come yet, but that it would be here the next day. If you currently own a home, then you know that banks typically provide a fifteen-day grace period to submit a mortgage payment before adding late fees. Well, it was the 14th day of the month. When thoughts came that didn't line up with the word of God, I just shut them down in the name of Jesus. I told the enemy to stop lying to me. I rebuked him in Jesus' name. Then, I confessed the word, believing that God would make a way.

One afternoon, faith came into fruition. My nephew arrived home from school. As he walked through the door, I handed him my keys for the mailbox and said, "Now, Adoniss, go to the mailbox and bring me back my check." I was just speaking in faith. My nephew came back and handed me the mail. I went through it slowly, and then I came across an envelope that was from my mortgage company. The front of the envelope looked like a check, but I couldn't wrap my mind around why the mortgage company would send us a check. I opened the mail and it was a fairly long piece of paper. It was a check! I almost passed out. The check was for twenty-three hundred dollars. I immediately dropped it on the table and ran through my house, praising God like I had lost my mind. My kids came running downstairs, thinking something had happened to me. I was expecting God to move, but I didn't expect Him to use my mortgage company to pay my mortgage. When I read the letter that accompanied the check, I discovered that we could just endorse the check and return it to them as payment on the mortgage. We apparently had surplus in escrow. Isn't God good? This in fact was a miracle! Oh, taste and see that the Lord is good. I love the verse in the bible that says the seed that is cast in good earth is when a person hears and takes in the good news, which allows them to produce a harvest beyond their wildest dreams. I believe that if I hadn't heard and acted on the word that Dr. Creflo Dollar shared, harvest would not have occurred. I heard the word and I put it to work. As a result, it produced harvest. The word of God didn't just get into my head, but it got into my heart. I believe it makes no sense for us to hear the word and not do what it says. We are only fooling ourselves according to James 1:22. Taking a step of faith in the right season is so important because most of us claim we are waiting on God. But most times, He is waiting on us. That's why having a daily life of prayer and reading God's word is so important. We can speak to the Father and He can speak to us.

The miracle of the mortgage company paying our mortgage didn't just happen once, but twice. I signed up for classes at Montgomery College and I had to pay my tuition out-of-pocket. My mortgage payment and all of the bills were due at the same time. We had some money saved up toward the mortgage payment, but I used some of it as a down payment for my tuition, which needed to be paid immediately. I knew I needed help financially, but this time, we didn't feel led to sow money.

Instead, we sowed the word of God into the atmosphere. Every time I became overwhelmed, I walked around my home, having a conversation with God, speaking His promises back to Him and declaring His word with confidence. I turned some praise and worship music on, and I worshipped God just for who He is. I felt a sense of the Holy Spirit in our home. I lifted my hands and just worshipped Him. I told God how good He is and how grateful I was to be His child. I walked in expectancy, waiting for Jehovah Jireh to move.

My daughter came home from school with the mail in her hands. She walked through the door while I was on the phone. She handed me the mail, which was one envelope from the mortgage company. I thought nothing of it. This time, it looked nothing like a check. I thought it was a request for payment of the mortgage. I slowly started opening it and, to my surprise, it was another check! This time, the check was for thirty-five hundred dollars and some change. I fell to the floor in amazement. No words could explain how I felt. God had done it again. The mortgage company had paid themselves yet again.

Then, I remembered sitting at the dinner table the night before and commanding in the name of Jesus that my mortgage company pay themselves again. I said, "Mortgage, go pay yourself right now, in the name of Jesus!" It obeyed; my mortgage company did indeed pay themselves. It worked because greater is He that is in me than he that is in world. If you are speaking death over your situation, begin to speak life today! *Death and life in the power of the tongue: and they that love it eat the fruit thereof* (see Proverbs 18.21). The word of God is life, so we must speak life.

Prayer is an essential weapon against the evil one. It is a Heavenly conversation with the Father. It is a way that believers connect with Him. Prayer allows us to have an intimate relationship with God. We seek His face and in the process, He reveals His will to us. According to the dictionary, the word conversation means an "informal interchange of thoughts or information." We must speak to our Heavenly Father through prayers. Then, we must set aside time for Him to speak to us through His spirit or through His Word. We must open our spiritual ears and heart so He can speak to us. Prayer is an important tool in every situation.

The bible says, in Matthew 7:7, *Ask, and it shall be given you; seek, and ye shall find; knock, and the door will be open unto you.* We must boldly go to the throne of grace and make our requests and needs known to God. Philippians 4:6-7 (NLT) admonishes us, *Don't worry about anything; instead, pray about everything. Tell God what you need, and thank him for all he has done. Then we will experience God's peace, we exceeds anything we can understand.* Our actions show that we have the peace of God. It is demonstrated when we totally lay aside all of our distress and leave it at the feet of the cross. Believers should pray and cast our cares on God because he cares for us (see 1 Peter 5:7).

Most believers don't know how to pray or what to say in the time of prayer. When we pray according to Romans 8:26-28 (NLT) the Holy Spirit helps us in our weakness. For example, we can find ourselves in the midst of so many perplexing things that we may not know what God wants us to pray for. *The Holy Spirit intercedes and prays for us in groaning that cannot be expressed in words: And the father who knows what the spirit is saying, for the spirit pleads for us believers in harmony with God's own will. And we know that causes everything to work together for the good of those who love God and are called according to his purpose for them.* We don't even have to pray in our own strength. We can lean and depend on Him for the words to say, even while we are praying.

The story of Anna is a perfect illustration that teaches us to pray without stopping. Luke 2:36 tells the story of Anna, a prophet who served God through fasting and praying night and day. She interceded and waited for the arrival of Jesus Christ. Anna not only prayed and waited, but she went around talking about the coming of Jesus. What she prayed for happened. When we pray to God according to 1 Thessalonians 5:16, we must always be joyful and never stop praying. When we walk by faith toward a harvest, prayer is our first step.

According to Mark 11:24, when we pray, if we believe we have received, then we have it. We must prepare ourselves to receive what we pray for. James 2:14, 17 (NLT) says, *What good is it, dear brothers and sisters, if you say you have faith but don't show it in your actions? Can that kind of faith save anyone? So you see, faith by itself isn't enough. Unless it produces good deeds, it is dead and useless.* Anna warred in the spirit for years, proclaiming the coming of Jesus Christ. Luke 2:38 says this great intercessor talked about the child to everyone, so much so that they also began to wait and expect the arrival of Jesus. She added action to her faith. She talked about what she believed was to come.

Just like Anna, after praying, we should talk about the expected outcomes of our situations and problems as if they have already happened. By faith, we can prepare ourselves by taking baby steps toward the harvest. In this stage, listening to the voice of the Holy Spirit is critical. Taking steps on our own can create Ishmael outcomes, so we have to make sure we are following the leading of the Holy Spirit. We are instructed to walk by faith, and not by what we see or what is going on around us. That's why I believe our actions, or a good deed, after we pray is a sure sign that we believe and trust in God. In spite of how crazy we may look to the naked eye, we should have the assurance that our prayer requests are granted.

I Samuel 25 tells the story of a beautiful and wise woman named Abigail. News came to Abigail that her husband and her whole household were in jeopardy of being killed by King David. Abigail, the bible says, used her faith. She worked and prepared food for David and his army. She flew into action, taking two hundred loaves of bread, two wineskins full of wine, sheep that had been slaughtered, nearly a bushel of roasted grain, one hundred clusters of raisins and two hundred fig cakes. She packed them on donkeys and told her servant, "Go ahead and pave the way for me." Abigail used the wisdom that God gave her and received favor from King David. The bible says that when Abigail saw the king, she got off her donkey and bowed low at his feet. She asked David to forgive her husband's trespasses, and he did. She saved her family's life. She additionally had such a great impact on David that when her husband passed away, David took her as his wife. This incredible woman used her faith and as a result, she found favor in the eyes of the king.

Like Abigail, Esther also used her faith and prepared herself before going in to see the king. In the book of Esther, Haman planned to destroy the Jews (Esther's people.) When Esther heard this news, she prepared herself by gathering all the Jews and her maidservants to fast and pray. She told the people, "Don't eat, or drink three days, night or day." She also fasted. She said, "I will go in unto the king." She knew going into the king could be very dangerous, but Esther said, "If I perish, I perish." Notice, that her process of preparation was fasting and praying. She was risking her life, but still she needed the king's favor. Favor came through employing her spiritual weapons.

The bible says, after the third day, Esther got dressed up in her royal robes and stood in the courts of the palace in the king's throne room. This was a leap faith because it was tradition that the King had to invite you to come into his courts. But Queen Esther relied on her faith in God. She placed her confidence and trust in the Almighty, who brings justice to His people. In Esther 5:2, we read, *And it was so, when the King saw Esther the queen standing in the court, that she obtained favor in his sight: and the King held out the golden scepter that was in his hands. So Esther drew near, and touched the top of the scepter.* In the end, she exposed the plan of Haman and she saved the life of her people by using her faith in God. Destiny was fulfilled because Queen Esther depended, trusted, committed to and prepared herself to receive a miracle from the Father. This is certainly uncommon favor.

Like Esther and Abigail, we should get ourselves in position to be ready to receive what God has already said. We should prepare ourselves by seeking the face of God and then moving when He says to move. I remember a time when a man of God called me and prophesied that I was going to be pregnant sooner than I thought. My husband and I were so excited. We prepared ourselves to receive what the man of God declared. The word says if we believe the prophet, we will prosper. Therefore, we took a step of faith and started purchasing baby clothes, blankets and baby bottles. To the natural eye, this may have appeared crazy or even a waste of time. The world, and even some believers, might think it is foolish to waste money on baby clothes since I wasn't pregnant in the natural just yet.

That's why I called this book *Krazy Faith.* I believed what the man of God said and what the God of the universe said shall be. I prepared to receive what was spoken. If God said it, then I believe it. My kind of faith causes me to act upon it.

Two years before that prophetic word, and shortly after I was saved, my sister called me and announced that she was engaged. The wedding would take place one year from the day she called me. I don't know what came over me, but all of a sudden, these words came out of my mouth, "I will come to your wedding with my husband." At that time, I wasn't seeing, talking to, nor did I even have anyone in mind to date or to marry. I just spoke those words in faith. As those words came out of my mouth, all I heard was silence, then laughter on the other end of the phone.

My sister asked, as she laughed, "You married? To who? You are not even dating anyone. You're the next Virgin Mary." Honestly, I did not know what to say, but I knew God was well able. When we believe God's word, we can boldly declare it freely. The word of God is seed. When God created the earth, He used seed (words) when He proclaimed, *Let there be light: and there was light* (see Genesis 1:3). Because the Father lives in us, we can also call those things which be not as though they were. Believers can speak forth the word of God boldly. Our Father gave us that authority. When we speak in our authority, we command the present and the future to be what God has already given us. My family asked me repeatedly about this husband that I had claimed I was going to marry. Each time, I responded, "Just like I said the first time, I will be attending the wedding with my husband." To my own surprise, those words that I spoke that day on the phone came to pass. Within a year, I met the most incredible man of my dreams. I wasn't even looking. He was sent by God. God blessed me, and he accompanied me to my sister's wedding. God granted my heart's desire and He didn't put me to shame. I received harvest on those seed words within a year.

I was even amazed at how God's word became flesh in my life just by speaking the word into the atmosphere. This changed my life. After that miracle, I became so careful of the words flowing out of my mouth because they have the power to shape lives. What have you been speaking? It's time to open the word of God and declare it over your situation until change comes. Look for harvest, prepare yourself to receive, and remember that God won't respond to your tears. His word says He collects our tears in a bottle (see Psalm 56:8). God's word moves Him. He has made an oath with Himself that He will keep every promise in His Word (see Hebrews 6). It is time to rise up, and declare the word!

Renowned preacher, teacher and author Bishop T.D. Jakes, Senior Pastor of The Potter's House in Dallas, TX, holds a huge annual conference called Woman Thou Art Loosed (WTAL). In 2012, I had the opportunity to attend that conference and it changed my life. This book was birthed through that great ministry. My mother-in-law called one day and asked if I was interested in attending the WTAL conference, which was being held in Atlanta, Georgia. I had heard so many good things about the WTAL conference, but I had never had a chance to attend. I didn't have a penny to my name, at that time, but I knew God was more than well able. I knew the whole trip had to be planned by faith.

I told my mother-in-law to put my name on the list for the church van. She told me she would pay for the hotel room, so all I needed to pay for was my plane ticket and my registration for the conference. As soon as I hung up the phone, I started looking for an airline ticket without knowing how I would pay for it. The ticket I found was manageable, but I still didn't have any money at that time to pay for it. I prayed and asked God to make a way. I went on the T.D. Jakes' ministry website and I viewed the information. But I still didn't have any money to pay for my registration at that time. I decided that I would pay for my registration for the conference when my husband got paid. However, payday came and after paying our bills, there was no money left over. I still trusted God.

Time went by so quickly, before I knew it, the conference was sold out. In addition, when I looked online, my airline ticket was nearly triple the original price. I started giving up, saying that maybe I shouldn't go. For some reason, my mother-in-law was still trying everything she could to persuade me to keep the faith. She told me she would ask around in church to see if anyone wanted to sell their ticket. When I got off the phone with her that day, my husband and I prayed again and we asked God to make a way. One week later, my mother-in-law called me again and said she found a ticket. I praised God for answering our prayers. I knew without a doubt that I belonged at that conference. Even though I needed a plane ticket, I knew if God made a way for the registration, He would make a way for my airline ticket.

My cousin came to visit me and before she left, I wanted to be a blessing to her. This was a step of faith because the only money we had was for our household bills. Yet again, it wasn't enough to pay all of our bills. So, my husband and I sowed a seed into her by faith. After we sowed, we prayed, calling harvest to come on our behalf. That very same week, we received an electronic deposited check into our bank account for eighteen hundred dollars. We then had enough to pay our bills and purchase my airline ticket to Atlanta. This was another miracle from God. He had made a way again, yet again. I praised Him, not because He blessed us with money, but because He is so awesome. Be encouraged and remember God is no respecter of a person. If He did it for me, He can do it for you. He is waiting on you to step out in faith.

If there is sickness in your body, the word of God says by His stripes, you are healed. It's already done! Matthew 8:17 says He took your sickness and removed all your diseases. It doesn't belong to you anymore. You don't have to pay for it. All you need is to accept what Jesus Christ did at Calvary and use your faith. This means you are healed already! It is time to accept your healing right now, in the name of Jesus! Stop begging God to heal you. The blood of Jesus has already completed the work. Accept your deliverance now. The Son of Man already finished the work over two thousand years ago. If God doesn't do anything else for us, He has done enough. Not only did He save us, but every morning when we wake up, it's a brand new day of grace and mercy.

Looking back on the conference, I can see why I had to be there. Every speaker had a word for me. It was a life-changing, powerful move of God. Things that I had been praying about for so long were answered at the conference. Pastor Sheryl Brady's message came with healing and restoration. The message came to remind me of God's promises. It came to heal my heart. The pain I felt about my barrenness had come to the surface yet again. When this woman of faith spoke, there were no dry eyes in sight. She came and reminded the women that God hadn't forgotten the promises He made. She reminded us that God was still going to do it. I wept like a two-year-old. Those words sunk directly into my heart because, for many years, I had become satisfied with my present state. I was satisfied with the children God blessed me with. I even stopped praying and asking God to bless my husband and me with a child of our own. When she spoke those words into the atmosphere, it dug up what I had buried away in my heart. I kept hearing her say, "God said He is still going to do it." There I was standing in the presence of thousands of women, but God was speaking directly to me. I left that conference restored. I felt as though I had to recommit myself totally to God's promises.

When WTAL was over, Bishop T.D. Jakes continued to tap into the power of the event through his message The Pecking Orders. He told the congregation for fifty-two days, he would meet us in the spirit in a time of devotion and prayer every morning. Because of these pecking orders, several women got together and started a WTAL prayer line. Every morning at 6 a.m., women from all over the country came together to pray. I decided to get up and push my way onto the prayer line. This also changed my life.

One morning, a prophet spoke directly into my life. She told me that my barrenness was not natural; it was spiritual. She told me that God was birthing forth ministry out of my barrenness and I would have a child from my husband's loins. I wept again like a baby because, after a decade of waiting, one word changed everything. All of a sudden, I saw growth in my pain and I took comfort in knowing that all that I was going through was not because of anything my husband or I had done. It was all God's plan. I was free! She freed me from all the shame and embarrassment I felt all those years. I was no longer in pain. I felt it was all now worth being gossiped about and laughed at. I again realized how blessed I was to have the opportunity to be used by God like this. I realized that God loves me and He wants to use me for His glory. I realized His plan was perfect.

Trusting God's plan is another step toward receiving harvest. The word trust (according to dictionary.com) means, "To have assurance or reliance on the character, ability, strength or truth of someone or something. One in which confidence is placed." God made a covenant with Abraham. He told him that he would be the father of nations. Abraham didn't focus on what he couldn't see; he kept his faith and trust in God's word. He didn't question God. He trusted God that it would come to pass. When we trust God, we don't look at what we see through our natural eyes. We can find rest when we trust in the Creator. According to Proverbs 3:5-6 (NLT), we must *trust in the Lord with all our hearts; do not depend on your own understanding. Seek his will in all you do, and he will show you which path to take.* When we trust God, it shows in what we say and how we react in every situation. If He closes a door, we can rest in knowing that He has our best interest at heart and He has a window open. For many years, I planned how I thought my life should go, but God's plan is perfect. I do believe He will make it worth my while. Through it all, I have learned to trust in God. I have learned how to wait. I have learned that my pain is not to harm me, but to bring me to a place where God can use me. 2 Timothy 2:12 says if we endure hardship, we will reign with Him.

The story of Ruth is an incredible story of faith, endurance, faithfulness and commitment. Ruth went through a heart-breaking period when her husband died. Naomi was Ruth's mother-in-law, who also suffered great loss when her two sons were killed and her husband died. In Ruth 1:5, when Ruth's husband died, she made a choice to stay faithful to Naomi. Ruth told her mother-in law she was committing herself to her until death. Her faith and faithfulness to Naomi was evident and it paid off in the end. Ruth put her faith to work. In Ruth 2:2 (MSG), she said, *I'm going out to glean among sheaves, following after some harvesters who will treat me kindly.* She knew Naomi's God as the one who would provide. Ruth found favor in the eyes of Boaz. Naomi instructed her on how to become desirable for Boaz and how to get him to notice her. Ruth took her mother-in-law's advice. She took a bath, put on perfume and dressed in her nicest clothes. Then, she went to the threshing floor. Naomi told Ruth not to allow Boaz to see her until he was finished eating and drinking. The wise woman told her to notice where he lied down, and then go and uncover his feet and lie down there. She did everything she was instructed to do, and because Ruth was obedient and committed, she obtained favor in her union with Boaz. She became a descendant in the line that gave birth to King David, whom Jesus Christ came through. When we trust and commit ourselves to God's plan, He can use us. If we submit ourselves to Him, generations to come will be blessed because of our obedience.

Submitting to the plan of God for our lives is essential. After we pray, we must prepare, trust and walk in thanksgiving. We must thank God in advance for the victory that is already won. Don't wait until you see victory, shout *now*! Psalm 107:1 (NLT) implores us to, *Give thanks to the Lord, for he is good! His faithful love endures forever.*

A while back, I had a strong desire to go back to school full-time. I lived in Virginia Beach and didn't have a car. Public transportation was very scarce. I woke up one morning and decided that I would step out on faith and apply for my classes without even knowing how I was going to get there. I believed by the time the semester started, that God would make a way. I received the application in the mail, filled it out and sent it back in with the application fee. I was accepted almost immediately. I started classes in the spring semester. God made a way. In the process of applying, I got married, so I used my new husband's truck to get to school. Talk about a double blessing! Over the years, I've been so thankful that God would use someone like me, who has just a little faith. I believe I'm a child of the Most High God, with absolutely no title behind my name, just believing and decreeing the word of God over situations in my life. I have seen the hand of God working in my life. I'm writing this book to encourage you to take God at His word. You too can see miracles, signs and wonders take place in your life. If you have been stuck in the same spot in your Christian journey, know that God has more for you. Just like Jesus told Peter, step out of the boat. But, don't be like Peter. Don't look at what is stirring around you. Keep your eyes on God, and He will lead you. Destiny is waiting on you. God is not finished with you!

Chapter 9
Waiting in Faith

James 1:2-8 (NLT) says, *Dear brothers and sisters, when troubles come your way, consider it an opportunity for great joy. For you know that when your faith is tested, your endurance has a chance to grow. So let it grow, for when endurance is fully developed, you will be perfect and complete, needing nothing. If you need wisdom, ask our generous God, and He will give it to you. He will not rebuke you for asking. When you ask Him, be sure that your faith is in God alone. Do not waver, for a person with divided loyalty is as unsettled as a wave of the sea that is blown and tossed by the wind. Such people should not expect to receive anything from the Lord. Their loyalty is divided between God and the world, and they are unstable in everything they do.*

These verses described how a believer should behave when they are going through a period of testing. During a period of testing, waiting is required. When we are in a period of waiting, our faith is being tested, our endurance is being developed and the trying of our faith is producing patience. The word wait means "to remain inactive or in a state repose, as until something unexpected happens." In the kingdom of God, waiting does not mean sitting around without doing anything. Prayer is always the first step because it's how believers communicate with the Father. Waiting teaches us patience, but it is not an easy thing to endure for most of us. We expect to receive everything in a hurry. Before coming to know Christ as my personal Savior and during the time I lived in Brooklyn, it was clear by driving in that city that no one likes to wait for anything, not even at the stoplight. When you are at the stoplight and it turns green, you better step on that gas; otherwise, you would definitely hear the sound of horns blowing. If you don't drive fast enough, you might be run over by a moving vehicle. I remember when my husband and I drove to Brooklyn for a funeral. When we left the funeral, we headed toward my sister's home. We stopped at a red light and before the light turned green, another driver ran into the back of our vehicle because of her impatience. Just like this example, we run into brick walls because we have no patience to wait on God's timing.

Psalm 27:14 says, *Wait on the Lord: be of good courage, and he shall strengthen thine heart: wait, I say, on the Lord.* God knew we would need His strength to keep waiting on Him. Therefore, when we have to wait, He offers us renewed strength. When we draw closer to His word, our strength will be renewed. When we wait on God to move, we lay aside our will and we totally rely on His will and plan. In waiting, we learn how to trust in him through prayer, devotional time, and we grow in God. God has the ultimate master plan. He has already planned our lives before the foundation of the world. He knows the beginning and the ending of our lives. Jeremiah 29:11 says, *For I know the thoughts that I think towards you, says the Lord, thoughts of peace, and not of evil, to give you an expected end.* God has good plans for His children, and we should rest in them. When we enter into His rest, we let go and give Him full authority to have His way.

If God closes a door, take no thought. He has another one opening just for you. If you are in a period of waiting, and it seems like nothing is happening, just know when the presence of the Lord shows up that your years of waiting will be well worth it. God wants to use you to bring glory to Himself. Keep waiting, praying and believing that all things will in fact work together for your good. Your weeping will last only for a night, but joy will come in the morning. Glory to God!

Be still in the presence of the Lord, and wait patiently for Him to act (see Psalm 37:7, NLT). In your waiting process, seek Him and get to know Him better. While you do this, your faith gets stronger and you become steadfast in birthing your purpose. Being impatient can cause you to miss your moment or make you do things that you might regret later. Sarah was impatient. While waiting on God, she tried to fix her own situation by allowing Abraham to sleep with Hagar, her Egyptian servant. In Genesis 16:1-2, she told Abraham that the Lord prevented her from having children. She said, *Go sleep with my servant. Perhaps I can have children through her.* Abraham agreed with Sarah's proposal. Hagar, the Egyptian servant, gave birth to a baby boy, Ishmael, in Genesis 16. She tried to rely on her husband's ability instead of relying on God's ability. God wants us to totally depend on Him. He doesn't want us to be independent, but we must be totally dependent on Him. Ishmael wasn't the son of promise, but God's promise was still fulfilled and Sarah gave birth to Isaac. God is always faithful, even when we are unfaithful.

Most of us find it difficult to wait on God's timing. A friend of mine missed her destiny because she didn't wait on God. For some strange reason, every time I visited her home, I knew something was wrong but I couldn't put my hands on what it was. Then, she shared her testimony with me. She told me she was in her late forties and she was raising three children as a single mom. None of the kids' fathers were paying child support and it was very difficult for her. She was introduced to a guy through a mutual friend, and they started dating. This young man was not saved, but he had a great job with benefits. He asked her to marry him. She said she had doubts, but she asked family members what they thought about it. The family members instructed her to go ahead and marry him. She said she felt in her heart it was the wrong thing to do, but she did it anyway.

Two years after she was married, she went back home for a visit and bumped into a gentleman from her past. They attended the same church, and she always thought he was the man she was supposed to marry. He was married, but when she ran into him on that visit, she found out that his wife had passed away. She felt as though she missed her opportunity to marry the man of her dreams. In fact, she believed he was her soul mate and she was stuck in a relationship with someone she didn't love.

Soon after our talk, she divorced and found herself right back in the same spot. My friend didn't wait on her appointed time. Because she was impatient, she missed her destiny. I love Isaiah 40:31 that says, *But they that wait upon the Lord shall renew their strength; they shall mount up with wings as eagles; they shall run, and not be weary; and they shall walk, and not faint.* Again, God promises us renewed strength if we wait on Him. If our strength is weak, we have to pursue renewed strength by plugging ourselves into God's word. If you find yourself walking and fainting, if you find yourself running and getting weary, it's time to examine your connection with the Father. When we wait on God, we can expect and look forward to His promises being fulfilled in our lives. In our time of waiting, we must spend time on our knees and in God's word.

There will be victory after this. The rain is here and your drought is over! Your anointing has increased, your faith has grown and your breakthrough is now!

Job 13:15 says, *Though he slay me, yet will I trust in him: but I will maintain mine own ways before him.* Job is an incredible example of how we should patiently wait on God. After losing everything, and having his body afflicted with boils, Job still trusted God. Job's wife told him to curse God and die, but instead he cursed the day he was born. Job 19:26 says, *And though after my skin worms destroy this body, yet in my flesh shall I see God.* During his turmoil, he still kept his eyes on God. He was speaking of Heaven; he was looking forward to putting away his earthly body and taking up his newly resurrected body.

Job was not looking at the things that he could see with his naked eyes. His eyes were fixed on the things that he could not naturally see. He had his heart and eyes fixed on his eternal home with his Father. As believers, we should take a great lesson from Job. We should trust God in every storm and season of turmoil in our lives. Most of us would have a hard time dealing with the hardships that Job had to endure. We would have given up and cursed God, or even slipped into depression or lost our minds. Job held on with everything he had. His faith was immovable. He believed in the one true and living God. In the end, when Job prayed for his friends in Job 42:10, and the Lord turned his situation around and he received twice as much as before. In the same way, if we can just fix our eyes on Jesus, we too can make it through every storm that comes our way. During our season of waiting, we must keep the faith in the Almighty. We must expect and wait on God's appointed time. Romans 10:8 say faith must be in our hearts and mouths. We must fill our hearts with the word, and then we must speak it with our mouths. We must wait in hope, be brave and be of good courage.

When I wrote this book, I had been married for almost twelve years. My husband and I were waiting for one of God's major promises to be fulfilled in our lives. It seemed like it was taking forever, but I know that this period of waiting was birthing forth ministry. Nevertheless, I believe God had already granted me my request the first time I prayed. During this time of waiting, I learned how to trust in God's timing. I no longer say, "If God does it…" Now I say, "When God does it…" During that period of waiting, my faith was also stretched and I became a different person than I was when I first came to Christ. My husband and I grew tremendously in our faith.

Faith allows me to keep hope alive, and my hope allows me to keep my faith alive. A very close friend of mine shared with me how he prayed for his father to accept Christ as his personal Savior for over twenty-two years. He had a very healthy and constant prayer life. His testimony encouraged me to be steadfast in my period of waiting, until I see the manifestation take place. It was all worth it because my friend's father accepted Jesus as his Savior before he passed away. In Galatians 6:9 (NLT), we are reminded to not get tired of doing what is good. In just the right time, we will reap a harvest of blessing if we don't give up. For twenty-two years, he held on to his faith in God, bending his knees for the salvation of his father. He could have grown tired and gave up, but God answered.

What are you waiting on today? How long have you been praying? The word of God says in Mark 11:24 that whatsoever you desire, when you pray, believe that you receive them and you shall have them. According to this verse, if we have a desire, and we pray and believe, we shall have what we ask for. The first time you prayed about your situation, the Father answered your prayers. While you wait, don't speak against what you believe. Get rid of unbelief by meditating on the promises of God, and then thank Him in advance for your breakthrough.

Sometimes after receiving the promises, God tests us to see if we will remain committed to Him. Abraham was already going to be the father of many nations to come, our father of faith. In Genesis 22, God tested Abraham to see where his loyalty lied. God told Abraham to build an altar and to sacrifice

Isaac as a burnt offering. Abraham took Isaac where God commanded him. Abraham picked up the knife and was about to kill his son as a burnt offering when the angel of the Lord called from heaven, saying, *"Abraham! Abraham!"*

"Yes." He replied, "Here I am."

"Don't lay a hand on the boy," the angel said. *"Don't hurt him in any way, for now I know that you truly showed you fear God. You have not withheld even your son, your only one."*

In Genesis 22:13, Abraham looked up and saw a ram, so he sacrificed it as a burnt offering in place of his son. This great man of faith remained committed to God even when he was asked to sacrifice Isaac, the child of promise. God provided a ram in the bush. Just like God provided for Abraham, He will provide and make a way for you. He will provide a ram in the bush. He will make a way for you when it seems like there is no way.

Chapter 10
Unmerited Favor

Grace is the unmerited favor of God, given to believers, according to Romans 12:3 (AMP). This means grace cannot be earned or bought. It is a gift given to us by our Heavenly Father when we receive Him as our personal Savior. 2 Peter 1:1 says, (NLT) *This faith was given to you because of the justice and fairness of Jesus Christ, our God and Savior.* It was given because of what Christ has done, which makes it possible for believers to inherit it. To the natural eye, many would say Abraham and Sarah didn't deserve to see the promise fulfilled. However, the word of God says Heaven and earth will pass away, but God's word remains the same. God's blessing to us depends totally on who He is and not who we are. There is nothing we can do or say that can make us earn God's blessing. It is purely a gift that our Heavenly Father gives us because of love. I always hear people saying, "Favor isn't fair." I totally agree with them because I believe God's favor upon His people is not based on us; it is based on Him. The ultimate testimony of God's favor and grace is when God accepts us into His family, regardless of past mistakes and failures. I have experienced God's favor and grace in my personal life. I remember several years ago, I had just married and my husband and I only had one vehicle. Our credit reports were messed up! My husband was active duty military personnel, and I was a full-time student. We only lived on one paycheck. Our paycheck was just enough to pay six hundred dollars in rent and put a little food on the table. Each of us came to the table with outstanding bills lingering on our credit. God blessed us, and my husband made rank; we decided to take a step of faith and walk into a car dealership and try to get a second vehicle. Before we even set foot in the dealership, we prayed and we asked God for His favor. We commanded angels to go ahead of us and prepare the right person to receive us.

When we stepped into the dealership, there was a saleslady waiting for us. By faith, we test drove a car. During our test run of the vehicle, we prayed and we declared that was our vehicle. When we made our way back into the car dealership, the saleslady had paperwork waiting for us. We filled out the paperwork and the saleslady pulled our credit reports. Then, something strange occurred. She started to ask us what each item on our reports was, and then she started to cross out each item saying it was paid in full. Then she went down our credit report and she marked paid across every bill that was outstanding. While doing this, I remember sitting in my seat in disbelief.

I knew that God was with us and He sent us to the right place at the right time, but I guess part of me was in disbelief and shock. When she was finished crossing out everything with paid in full, we followed her into her boss' office. He looked at the credit report and then asked the saleslady, "What are all these items that are crossed out with paid in full? Did they pay all these items?" She said, "Yes." Before my husband and I could say anything, the saleslady conducted the conversation with her boss. We walked out of that dealership with a very reliable vehicle that we still have today. Glory to God in the highest! I believe without a shadow of a doubt that God's favor was with us that day. Once we activate our faith, we can experience God's favor.

The Gentile woman in Matthew 15:21 received God's unmerited favor. She wasn't a believer, but she had great faith. She had persistent faith. The word persistent means, "the act of persisting. To do something, or try something consistently until progress is made." This woman's daughter was possessed by demons, which tormented her severely. She came to Jesus pleading with Him, *"Have mercy on her son of David."* Jesus gave her no reply, not even a word. The disciples even urged Jesus to turn her away because they said that she was bothering them with her begging. Then Jesus said to the woman that He was only sent to help God's sheep who are the people of Israel. Still, in her persistence, she came again worshipping him, and pleading, *"Lord, help me."*

Again, He said, *"It isn't right to take food from the children and throw it to the dogs."*

Then the woman replied, *"That's true, Lord, but even dogs are allowed to eat the scraps that fall beneath their master's table."* Jesus responded, *"Dear woman, your faith is great, your request is granted."* Her daughter was instantly healed.

This woman wasn't about to give up on her breakthrough. When I first read this chapter, I thought, *"Why would Jesus turn away a woman that needed His help?"* I didn't even understand why He told her that He was only sent for God's sheep who are the children of Israel. But, Jesus knew this woman before she said a word. He was testing this woman's faith. The Holy Spirit led me to Colossians 1:26-28, which says, *Even the mystery which hath been hid from ages and from generations, but now is made manifest to his saints. To whom God would make known what are the riches of the glory of this mystery among the Gentiles; which is Christ in you, the hope of glory. Whom we preach, warning every man, and teaching every man in all*

wisdom; that we may present every man perfect in Christ Jesus.
Here is how the Message version breaks this down: *God wanted
everyone, not just Jews, to know this rich and glorious secret
inside and out regardless of background regardless of their
religious standing. The mystery in a nutshell is just this. Christ is
in you, so therefore you can look forward to share in God's glory
- it's that simple.* Therefore, we can draw from these verses that
it doesn't matter who you are. The good news of Christ is for
everyone. We can say that this woman's persistent faith was
being tested and because she went through and held on during
her testing time, she had the victory.

I also received God's undeserved favor one holiday season
when my husband and I placed two sets of Christmas gifts on
layaway at a department store. When we opened the layaway, we
paid the minimum amount due. Two weeks later, another
payment was due, but my husband and I couldn't afford to make
a payment. We trusted that God would make a way. By faith, I
went on the store's website, viewed the layaway policy and
called to ask if they could hold our layaway for another week.
The woman on the phone agreed. I hung up the phone, thanking
God in advance for the provision to take it out. Payday came and
I still couldn't afford the layaway payment, but I knew I needed
to get the layaway out because Christmas was a week away.
After the bills were paid, I looked in the bank and it looked like

we could only afford to get one set of items out. Both of the layaways totaled four hundred dollars.

My husband and I discussed the possibility putting one layaway back for another time. We decided to go to the department store. On our way there, we started praying. We decreed that all of our needs were met according to His riches in glory. Then I thought about what God says in Hebrews 11:6. I knew God would not go back on His promises and His word would not return empty.

When we got to the layaway section at the store, a couple was waiting in line. I could tell because of the look on their faces that they weren't happy. I stood in line and waited my turn. I handed the cashier our first receipt and she told us how much it was. I gave her my debit card and she processed the payment. When that was finished, I gave her my second receipt and she told me that I owed a penny.

I didn't understand. I looked at my husband and he looked back at me. There was only one problem—neither of us had a penny.

The cashier told us not to worry about the penny as she went to retrieve our layaway.

Apparently, someone had made a payment online for the layaway. When we received our layaway, we noticed that something needed to be returned so we made our way to the customer service desk in front of the store. While standing in line, many crazy thoughts went through my mind. I thought the devil was setting us up to be arrested for stealing. While having these thoughts, a lady standing in the back of the line said all of a sudden, "Oh it's crazy in layaway right now because some Secret Santa came and paid off several people's layaways. People coming in to pick up their layaway and finding they owed one penny on their layaway. I wish that was me." I felt overwhelmed! I then knew that God used this Secret Santa to be a blessing to my family. God never makes a mistake. He knows what to do every time.

I was happy the layaway was paid off, but mostly, I hoped to be the one to bring joy to people who were in need. God is awesome! Not because He paid off my layaway, but because of His unconditional love for His people. He is everything we need!

Over two thousand years ago, Jesus paid the ultimate price and released everything a believer needs for life and godliness (see 2 Peter 1:3). We will see life at its fullest when we surrender ourselves to God's will through our faith in Him. By faith, we live our lives one day at a time and if we allow the Holy Spirit to lead and guide us all of the time, there will be no defeat.

I remember needing six hundred and eighty dollars in order to put braces on my nephew's teeth. First, I cancelled his appointment because I didn't have the money for the down payment. I rescheduled the appointment, believing that God would make a way. His appointment was on a Monday, but

Friday came and I didn't see the money. I thought I should call again and cancel the appointment, but for some strange reason, the day came and went and I totally forgot to do just that. I prayed and thanked God for making a way. I knew that something needed to happen because the time had run out and I couldn't call and cancel the appointment because they would charge me for not showing up. Monday morning came and there was no money in sight. All through the morning, I kept thanking God for making a way. I asked God what He would like me to do. I told Him I needed Him to make a way before three o'clock. As the day went on, I thanked Him and praised Him for His faithfulness. When I was finished praying, I closed my mouth and listened for instructions.

The Holy Spirit instructed me to call the orthodontist's office at two o'clock and tell them I wanted to set up a payment plan. I asked, "Lord, how would this be possible because three years ago, I used the same orthodontist's office for my son's braces and they told me I needed to pay the first initial payment upfront because that was their policy?" I had no idea how it was going to work out, but I trusted what God directed me to do. Two o'clock came and I walked over to the phone, with my legs shaking and my fingers sweating with nervousness. I picked up the phone and dialed the number slowly. I opened my mouth and stuttering words began flowing slowly. The female voice on the other end said, "Hello, how may I help you?"

I said, "Hello yes, how are you? My name is Maxine and my nephew has an appointment at three o'clock today and I just would like to know if it's any way possible if I can break up the initial payment into two payments?"

Immediately, the woman said, "Sure, that won't be a problem at all. I will have the contract ready for you when you get here."

I said, "Thank you so much. See you soon." As soon as I hung up the phone, I started praising God for His goodness. I couldn't believe it was that easy. I felt as though the woman on the phone was waiting for me to call. Just as the Holy Spirit had spoken, it had all worked out.

When I got to my appointment, another receptionist called me into a room to sign the contract. She then asked for a check. I stated in a calm voice, "I spoke to Laura and she told me it was okay if I call in Friday to make my first payment."

The receptionist said, "I'm sorry, but that's not our policy." She asked me if I could postdate a check for Friday. I didn't have my checkbook with me, and I felt bad because I didn't want anyone to get into trouble. I called my husband and I asked him if he could bring my checkbook to the orthodontist's office, which was located across the street from our house. He agreed. I told the receptionist my husband was on his way to bring my checkbook. When my husband arrived, I wrote the postdated check. As I handed the check to the receptionist, she said,

"Mama, that's fine. You don't have to postdate a check. You can just call in the payment Friday." Then all of a sudden, I heard the Holy Spirit saying, "I never said write a check, did I?" I quickly repented for not following His direction, yet I thanked Him for His favor and grace. When I walked out of that office, I realized that most times, we ask God for money when all we need is His unmerited favor. God gives us favor, not because we have been good or because we do everything right, but because He loves us so much. We don't have to be perfect, nor do we have to look perfect or have a perfect background. All that qualifies us is by faith we received Him into our hearts and accept His perfect gift. The bible says if we confess with our mouths and believe in our hearts that Jesus is Lord, we are saved by grace. That's what qualifies us to receive His unmerited favor.

Here is a woman who received undeserved favor because of her good deed. 1 Kings 3:16 (NLT) says, *Sometime later, two women came in to King Solomon to have an argument settled. One said, please, my Lord, "This one woman and I live in the same house. I gave birth to a baby while she was with me in the house. Three days later, this woman also had a baby. We were alone; there were only two of us in the house, but her baby died during the night when she rolled over on it. Then she got up in the middle of the night and took my son from beside me while I was asleep. She laid her dead baby in my arms and took mine to sleep beside her.* King Solomon asked God for great wisdom so he could lead his people and distinguish between right and wrong. So he decided to cut the baby in half. (I believe this was to test the loyalty of both women.) By faith, the real mother of the child wanted to save her baby's life. She asked the King Solomon to give the baby to the other mother, whose baby was dead. The woman whose baby was dead wanted Solomon to cut the baby in half. Solomon decided to keep the baby alive and gave it to the mother who wanted to save his life. One may argue, "Some people have faith; others have good deeds." But I say, "How can you show me your faith if you don't have good deeds? I will show you my faith by my good deeds?" The woman was willing to give up her baby in order to keep it alive. As a result, her baby's life was spared and the king returned the baby to her. Again, we see God's unmerited favor being demonstrated. When we choose righteousness, He blesses us beyond measure.

In fact, when we choose to worship Him in spite of what we see, we tell God by our actions that we surrender everything to Him. Then, He can come in and work out everything for His glory and our good. He is the God of the mountaintop and valley. With our hands lifted up, and our hearts focused on Him through every situation, He can perform miracles, signs and wonders.

David also received God's unmerited favor when he used his faith to slay Goliath in 1 Samuel 17. Samuel went to the house of Jesse because God told him to anoint one Jesse's sons as the next king of Israel. Jesse brought out all of his sons, who were of great stature, to face Samuel, but the Lord did not choose any of them. Jesse then told Samuel that he had a young son who watches over sheep and goats. When David came into the presence of Samuel, the Lord told Samuel to anoint him as the next king of Israel. God saw and knew the heart of David, and he found favor over his brothers.

Then by faith, David went against Goliath in 1 Samuel 17. Goliath taunted the Israelites. He requested that one man from the Israelite army come down and fight him. However, when Saul and the Israelite army heard this, they all were terrified and deeply shaken. Goliath told the Israelites if he won the battle, they would be slaves to the Philistines. David wasn't afraid of the challenge at all. He didn't allow Goliath's size or reputation to intimidate him one bit. He wasn't afraid to fight Goliath. He was used to going against animals, creatures and things that were bigger and stronger then he was. He had the victory of defeating a lion and a bear under his belt. He had faith in God. David knew all that he had to do to be used by God was to be available. According to 1 Samuel 17:37 (NLT), David said, *The Lord who rescued me from the claws of the lion and the bear will rescue me from the Philistine.* As soon as Goliath saw David, he looked at him as the boy he was and saw no inner strength.

David told Goliath, "You come to me with sword, spear and javelin, but I come to you in the name of the Lord of Heaven's

Armies. The God of the armies, whom you have defiled, today the Lord will conquer you, and I will kill you and cut your head off. Then I will give the dead bodies all of your men to the birds and wild animals, and the whole world will know that there is a God of Israel! And everyone assembled here will know that the Lord rescued his people, but not with sword and spear. This is the Lord's battle and he will give you to us!" David spoke words of faith to Goliath. By faith, he told him exactly what was going to occur before it manifested in the natural. These are words of declaration. He declared victory in advance. I can only imagine the look on Goliath's face when David, the shepherd boy, was talking to him. He probably was thinking, *"Yeah right, shepherd boy. You're cutting what head off?"* David had great confidence in God; his confidence was not in Saul's armor that couldn't fit his body nor was his confidence in a great weapon. David tapped into his inner strength. He found strength in the one who lived in him. He found strength in the one and only true God, El Shaddai!

David put action to his declaration by reaching into his shepherd's bag, taking out a stone, and hurling it with his sling, hitting the Philistine in the forehead. The stone sank in and Goliath stumbled and fell on his face to the ground. David triumphed over the Philistine with only one stone and a sling. I have heard this story so many times, but even now, I can imagine the faces of the soldiers when they saw their great champion defeated by a boy without any "mighty weapons." In fact, I would love to have seen the faces of King Saul and David's oldest brother, Eliab, who thought he was in way over his head. Eliab thought David was prideful. But, he didn't know his little brother possessed the power of God. He didn't know this shepherd boy had tapped into unmerited favor and could put his faith in action to slay the giant. David made himself available to be used by God and because he did, he obtained victory for the children of Israel. David moved from faith to faith. He killed the lion, the bear and eventually, Goliath.

We can also slay the giant (or giants) in our lives and receive favor in every situation. Every situation that seems impossible is an opportunity for us to learn how to take a step of faith and move toward victory, just like David. We can also conquer our Goliath by not looking to people for deliverance, but looking to the One True Deliverer (Jehovah Yahweh). We are more than conquerors according to Romans 8:37. God gives us the ability to solve problems. David recognized that the spirit who lives in him was greater than Goliath was. He realized who he was in God. The stature of this boy was not important at all; what was important was that he was a vessel, ready to be used by God. David won the battle because he knew that greater was living on the inside of him. Once believers realize the One inside of us is greater than anything in this world, we too can go up against Goliath and win every time. In Romans 8:11 (NLT), the bible says, *The spirit of God, who raised Jesus from the dead, lives in you.* Again, David could have been afraid just like everyone else, but instead he trusted in knowing that the God he served was well able to deliver. David used action with his faith, and in the end, he gained victory for his people. He had krazy faith!

Chapter 11
Lifeless Faith

James 2:17 says, *Even so Faith, if it hath not works, is dead, being alone.* I remember when I got saved and I was in a dire need of a car. Living in Brooklyn, I had no need for a car because public transportation was dependable. However, moving to Virginia, I had no choice but to get a car because public transportation was scarce. I went to several car dealerships and none of them approved me for a vehicle because of my credit history. I was also a single parent who only made minimum wage. After going to several dealerships, I got tired and I completely gave up. One Sunday, my pastor spoke a word to me directly from God. He said, "The Lord said He is going to bless you with a new car within seven days." I was so excited! I couldn't believe it was finally going to happen. I was a babe in

Christ, and I had no idea about faith. I thought since God said He was going to bless me with a car that I could stop searching. I thought God would just drop the car out of the sky. I thought He would lay it on someone's heart to give me a car. Six days went by and I still didn't have a car. On the seventh day, I got upset with God because I felt as though He hadn't kept His word. I even felt that maybe the pastor got it wrong.

This was the same pastor who had prophesied to the church earlier that someone would be stripped of everything. Little did I know, it was me. I hadn't realized that my faith was lifeless because there was not action with it. The seventh day came and went, and I had not received my car. I missed my opportunity to be blessed because my faith was dead. I hadn't put any works to what I believed. Many times, we know what it is to have faith but some of us don't see harvest because we fail to add work to our faith. As a result, we live our Christian lives without ever seeing manifestation of God's promises. Then, we get upset with God because we feel He's not doing what He said He would do.

The problem is with us, not with God. We are the reason why we can't see manifestation take place. Some of us get too lazy and we don't want to add work to our faith. The bible makes it clear. Faith without works is dead. I am not saying you should solely depend on your own strengths and abilities. Follow the guidance of the Holy Spirit and allow Him to lead you. When we try to do things on our own strength, we produce trouble and heartaches. So, seek God and let Him lead you. If you are sitting around waiting on God, most times, He is waiting on you. He has already accomplished it. The minute you prayed, He gave it to you. Greater is He that is in you than he who is in this world. It's time to pick up your mat and walk.

Let's look at the story of the lame man in John 5. This man was paralyzed and sick on the porch surrounding the Pool of Bethesda for 38 years. One day, Jesus was passing by. He told the man that He was aware of his illness and asked him, *"Do you want to get well?"*

"I can't Sir," the sick man said. *"For I have no one to put me in the pool when the water bubbles up. Someone else always gets there ahead of me."*

Jesus told the man, "Stand up, take up your mat, and walk!"

Instantly, the man was healed! He rolled up his sleeping mat and began walking! This man had been sick for 38 years, lying at the pool for many years, waiting for someone to put him in the water. The lame man's faith was lifeless. He was comfortable in his situation. He hadn't attempted to put himself into the water to be healed, so he waited. Thank God that Jesus was passing by and is rich in compassion and love. This man received healing because of who Jesus is, not because he deserved it. God has given many of us a vision, but we are waiting on a get-rich-quick scheme in order to get started or we are waiting on Him to drop the money out of the sky. Zechariah 4:10 says, *We must not despise small beginnings, for the Lord rejoices to see the work begin.* We should start where we are. Small plants will eventually grow into tall trees. Being obedient to God pleases Him. Proverbs 13:11 (NLT) says, *Wealth from a get rich scheme quickly disappears.* This kind of wealth does not last forever. All believers must use their faith. In every situation, faith is the driving force that is required to see destiny fulfilled. This man was comfortable in his environment and his situation. His sickness lasted much longer than it had to. His faith was lifeless because he didn't attempt to put himself in the pool and it had no action. We should accept what Jesus has done and use our faith in order to live a victorious life.

When we take our mind off God and place it on our situations, doubt steps in. We become shipwrecked, just like Peter when he stepped off the boat and began walking toward Jesus. He shifted his focus to the storm around him. Because Peter took his eyes off Jesus, he started doubting and he found himself sinking. *Jesus asked Peter, "You of so little faith, why did you doubt me?"* Peter still had faith, but when he started looking at the storm around him, he stepped into unbelief. We can have faith, but still walk in unbelief or, as Jesus said, doubt.

In Mark 9:17-18 (NLT), Jesus was teaching amongst many gathered when a man in the crowd spoke up, *"Teacher, I brought my son so you could heal him. He is possessed by an evil spirit that won't let him talk. It throws him violently to the ground. Then he foams at the mouth and grinds his teeth and becomes rigid."*

He asked the disciples to cast out the evil spirit, but they couldn't do it. In Mark 9:22, the boy's father begged Jesus, *"Have mercy on us and help us, if you can."* Jesus responded in a question, *"What do you mean, if I can? Anything is possible if a person believes."*

The father cried out, "I do believe, but help my unbelief!"

When Jesus saw that the crowd of onlookers was growing, he rebuked the evil spirit. The man asked Jesus to help him overcome his unbelief, but not once did Jesus tell the man that he had no faith. This man had enough faith to come to Jesus and ask Him to heal his son, even after the disciples could not. That man's faith wasn't the question; his unbelief was. When we're walking in unbelief, doubt and worry come in and rob us of manifestation. We have to get rid of unbelief in order to see God's glory in our lives.

God showed me that I was also walking in unbelief one day during my time of testing. In the course of life, my husband and I were having a really hard week. It started with our brakes needing repair, and then the sensor light in the car came on. As if that wasn't enough, my truck had a flat tire. We ordered two new tires to replace the worn ones that caused the flat. When we got the truck back, the mechanic told my husband that one of the rims was bent.

Every time we drove the truck, the wheels shook out of control. If that wasn't bad enough, my husband and I were stopped several times by other drivers, warning us that our tires were shaking. He then was pulled over by a police officer, warning him to get the tire fixed. Because we had spent three hundred dollars on new tires, we couldn't afford to do anything else at that time. I felt so overwhelmed with everything. I managed to get myself together, and I attempted to praise and worship God in hopes that would make me feel a little better. But as I walked into the kitchen, opened the fridge, freezer and cabinets, and saw that there was no food, my mood became somber again. There was also no money in our bank account.

The tears started to flow. Doubt stepped in and I found myself asking God questions like, "God, where are you? I have needs to be fulfilled." It was so hard to get a prayer through. It became difficult to stand on God's word and, for some reason, fear and worry stepped in and it was hard to think about past blessings and victories. I managed to walk myself over to the phone and call a friend. I needed encouragement. I needed to hear the truth of God's word. I called a good friend and the minute she heard my voice, she knew what I needed. I started talking and she said, "You don't go any further. Don't even start talking crazy. You don't want to cancel out your blessing.

Remember your words." I told her how it made me feel, having to call and ask my mom for financial help. The next thing that came out of her mouth slapped me in the face.

She said, "At least you can call your mother for help. My mother and father are dead, and I can't call either one of them." Those words cut deeply into my heart. My worries, fears and frustrations all disappeared. I tried to pull myself together so I could be an encouragement to my friend. Then she spoke again, "At least you can pay your mortgage every month." This was another slap in the face. I was beginning to realize how blessed I was to have my mother and to have money to pay the mortgage every month. When I hung up the phone, I repented to God for failing Him again. I prayed and interceded on behalf of my friend.

I knew I had faith and I knew how to step out on faith. But I wasn't sure what had happened. God answered me when I was watching Christian television later on that night. He showed me what happened through Dr. Creflo Dollar, who was speaking on unbelief. I knew instantly that God had led me to turn my television on just in time. He was speaking directly to me. While listening to him, the Holy Spirit replayed everything that happened earlier that day in slow motion. Then I realized unbelief was stirred up when I opened my cabinet and fridge.

Even though I had witnessed miracles and favor time and time again throughout my life, I had unbelief present in my heart. Walking in unbelief is serious. It shuts the hands of God from working on your behalf. Yes, God loves us and He is rich in grace and mercy; however, our actions can show that we don't trust Him to do what He said He would do. My husband and I firmly believe in sowing and reaping. There were times when I planted a seed and nothing happened. When I went to God to ask what happened to the increase, He revealed to me that I often strangled my seed. One thing I loved about Dr. Creflo Dollar's message is that he took time to teach about overcoming unbelief. He said, "We must find God's promises that pertain to every situation in our lives, and we must meditate on God's word day and night." Declaring the word of God over every situation puts our minds at ease. That's why God instructed us to hide His word in our hearts so we won't sin against Him (see Psalm 119:11). If you're struggling right now with unbelief, it is time to be free today. When worry, doubt and fear come, shut them down with the word; simply meditate on God's promises. You will then see your life totally transformed into freedom.

In Exodus 16, God took the children of Israel out of bondage in the land of Egypt and led them into the wilderness. They saw God using Moses to demonstrate miracles, yet they still murmured and complained. God took them out of Egypt and through the Red Sea. He parted the sea to reveal dry ground, with walls of water on each side, yet they weren't convinced that He was able to deliver them. He fed them manna from Heaven each day, yet still they walked in unbelief and disobedience. They even looked back and wished they were still in Egypt.

They complained, saying God brought them out of Egypt to starve them to death. God had set them free, fed them every day, but they still weren't thankful. They failed every test God put them through. They disregarded every instruction that He gave them each day. In Exodus 16:4, (NLT) the Lord told Moses, *"Look, I'm going to rain down food from heaven for you. Each day the people can go out and pick up as much food as they need for that day."* He said to Moses, *"I will test them in this to see whether or not they will follow my instructions."* They disobeyed what God instructed and kept some food for the next morning. Because of that, God allowed the manna to be overcome with maggots and it had a terrible stench.

Just like the children of Israel murmured and complained against God, we also murmur and complain against Him. Often, God brings us out of situations, yet we wish to go back to the place or point that we were delivered from. In addition, God shows us favor and grace, yet we still have trouble trusting in His will. When God gives us specific instructions, we do the opposite. Then we get angry with God because we think He's not moving fast enough. The children of Israel held up their own destiny. In fact, many of them died in the wilderness and they never got to see The Promised Land.

Our God is a just God. Even though our God is just, we should not take His love for us for granted. We should make a decision today to stop murmuring and complaining, and to commit ourselves to trust in, believe in and obey His word. Our decision today can move us into a season of harvest and eventually, lead us into our destiny. Ask God to forgive you for not trusting in Him. Ask Him to show you how to stop murmuring and complaining. Make a decision to have time set aside each day for prayer and devotion. Ask Him for the strength to seek His face diligently. Start by declaring the word of God through every storm and situation of your life. Always remember the story of the children of Israel. They delayed their own destiny because of their disobedience, murmuring and complaining. *Trust in the Lord with all your heart; and lean not to your own understanding. In all thy ways, acknowledge Him, and He will direct your paths* (see Proverbs 3:5-6)

We also have lifeless faith when we fail to do what God has commanded us to do. The word of God declares in Hebrew 7:7 (NLT), *And without question, the person who has the power to give a blessing is greater than the one who is blessed*. It is better to give than to receive. When we give, great joy comes from meeting the needs of others. Our faith is dead when we choose not to do what the word of God has commanded us to do. The tenth of everything we earn belongs to God. He is the one who gives us the ability to earn it. The greatest joy comes from meeting the needs of others.

Malachi 3:10-11 says, *Bring ye all the tithes into the storehouse, that there may be meat in mine house, and prove me now herewith, said the Lord of hosts, if I will not open the window of heaven, and pour you out a blessing, that there shall not be room enough to receive it. And I will rebuke the devourer for your sakes, and he shall not destroy the fruit of your ground; neither shall your vine cast her fruit before the time in the field, saith the Lord of hosts.*

God loves us, and His love for us is never conditional; however, when we don't sow our tithes and offerings, we don't receive the fullness of the blessings that God intends for His children. It takes faith and trust in God to tithe. We sow our tithes unto the Lord because it's another way for us to say, "Thank you Lord for blessing us with the ability to earn it." How could we *not* want to thank God for making provision for us? The season where I had to decide whether to pay my rent or to pay my tithes wasn't easy at all. It is through that season of my life, however, that I learned how to trust God. Regardless of what is going on, I must sow my tithes. It really doesn't matter how important it was to pay my rent. God is my source. He wanted me to trust and depend on His provision. Even though I lost my little two-bedroom apartment, God has blessed me abundantly today, just as He promised. You cannot afford *not* to sow your tithes.

Ten percent of your income belongs to the Lord, and there is no compromise. Make a decision right now that today is the best day to begin to obey God and stop walking in disobedience to His word. I grew up hearing many excuses about why some people didn't sow their tithes. Many were concerned with the pastor using the money for his personal gain. Depending on the type of car the pastor drives or the house he lives in, many feel like he may be 'stealing money' from the church. These are lies that come directly from the accuser of the brethren (the devil). 1 Peter 5:8 (NLT) says, *Watch out for your great enemy, the devil. He prowls around like a roaring lion, looking for someone to devour.* The devil is a deceiver and he accuses God's people.

I'm not here to tell you that these kinds of things have never happened before. One thing I know for sure is that God is judge and jury. We have no right to allow the devil to accuse a great man or woman of God. I do believe that the enemy blinds people so they can't see the truth. We sow our tithes unto the Lord because in the end, it's between us and God, not the woman or man of God. What really matters is our obedience to the Father. If you're not sowing your tithes because you feel like you don't have enough, it's time to renew your mind with the word of God. If your mind is renewed, your way of thinking will change.

Ask God to lead you through His word. Make a decision that when He shows you His will, you will not ignore what He's leading you to do next. I guarantee you will move from living a life of little faith to living a life of possibilities. When we sow our tithes and offerings, the windows of Heaven are open to us. In fact, 2 Corinthians 9:8 (NLT) says, *And God will generously provide all you need. Then you will always have everything you need and plenty left over to share with others.* Our offering multiplies when we sow it into the kingdom. Here is a prayer for you! *Father I pray for every person who is reading this book, who is struggling with trusting You in their tithes and offering. I pray that these words would move them to seek you and they will become tithes giver. I thank you in advance Father that they are moving to another level in you. In advance, we give you glory and praise, In Jesus' name. Amen.*

Achan failed to obey God in Joshua Chapter 6. God told Joshua after the people took the city that everything in it should be accursed and set apart as an offering to the Lord. He told Joshua not to take anything set apart for destruction because whoever did, would be destroyed and doing so would bring trouble to the camp of Israel. The only thing or person God told Joshua to bring out of Jericho was Rahab, the prostitute, and the others in her household. This is because she protected the spies. Achan disobeyed God in Joshua 7 and removed some of the things that were set apart for destruction and hid them in his camp. God became very angry with the people of Israel. A curse was proclaimed against them. God told Joshua to command the people to purify themselves because what they picked up made them unholy. He said, *"They will not be able to defeat their enemies until they remove that thing that was a curse from among them."*

In Joshua 7:19, Joshua confronted Achan and asked him to tell the truth about what he had done. Achan admitted he had sinned against the Lord. Then Joshua and all the Israelites took Achan and everything he had, including his family members, animals and the accursed things and they bought them down into the valley of Achor. All the Israelites stoned Achan and his family and burned their bodies. Because Achan disobeyed God, he not only lost his life, but his family was also destroyed. Achan's ultimate price was his life and his future generations because of his disobedience.

Our disobedience causes destruction. Eli was a great priest in the tabernacle of the Lord in 1 Samuel 1:9. Eli had two sons, Hophni and Phinehas, and they were priests in the house of the Lord. The sons of Eli did evil in the Lord's eyes; they committed very serious sins in the Lord's sight. Eli was very old, but he was aware of what his sons were doing to the people of Israel. He talked to them and told them to stop what they were doing, but he failed to discipline them. The Lord had already planned to put them to death. He gave them another warning, but they still didn't take heed. Judgment came to Eli and his house. Eli's sons were stripped of their duties in the tabernacle and they could no longer serve as priests. In addition, because they did wrong in the sight of the Lord, the members of Eli's family died before their time. None of them reached old age.

God told Eli that He would prosper the people of Israel, but his family would not be prosperous and both of his sons would die on the same day. Even though Eli was warned, he failed to bring corrections to his sons. God was angry with Eli because he failed to punish his sons and correct their behavior. Just as the Lord had promised, Israel was at war with the Philistines, and both of Eli's sons were killed in battle the same day. Also, the Philistines defeated Israel and they took the Ark of the Covenant of the Lord into captivity. Eli learned that his sons were killed and of the news about the Ark of the Covenant. When he did, Eli fell backwards from his seat beside the gate and broke his neck and died. In 1 Samuel 4:18, we discover not only did Eli and his sons die, but when his daughter-in-law learned of everything that happened, she went into labor and died in childbirth. When we fail to obey God, our disobedience can be felt for generations to come. It is so important that we do a heart check and that we don't take what God has done for us lightly as a way to stay in sin. Eli's light went dim and he needed to plug himself into the source in order to recommit himself back to God.

It is time for us to do a heart check. Make sure your light hasn't gone dim. Ask God to do surgery on your heart and remove everything that is contrary to His word. Ask Him to make your light brighter. Ask Him to restore you back to your rightful place in Him. By faith, receive His forgiveness--right now. According to 1 John 1:9, the word of God says, *God is faithful and just to forgive us of our sins and cleanse us from all unrighteousness.* Hallelujah!

Chapter 12
Faith Requires Believing and Receiving

In many situations and in the lives of many believers, we don't get answers to our prayers because we have problems believing and receiving what God has said in His word. Let us take look at the story of Elijah in 1 Kings 18. He believed God. God told Elijah the drought was over and the rain was coming. Elijah received what God said and thus, he saw manifestation. He prepared himself by asking his servant to go look over the mountain. The servant went to look seven times and on the seventh time, he saw a little cloud about the size of a man's hand. The word of God says, *So shall my word goeth forth out of my mouth: It shall not return on to me void, but it shall accomplish that which I please, but it shall accomplish that which it please, and it shall prosper in the thing whereto I sent it* (see Isaiah 55:11). We can rest assured that whatever God has said, it will come to pass. However, to see manifestation take place in our lives, first, we must believe, receive and have total confidence in the word of God.

Mark 11:23 (NLT) says, *I tell you the truth, you can say to this mountain, "May you be lifted up and thrown into the sea," and it will happen. But, you must really believe it will happen and have no doubt in your heart.* One day as I was watching TV, I came across a show, *How Has Lottery Changed My Life?*

One lady on the show who won the lottery was in her late 40s. This story touched me because while listening to it, I saw faith in her action. Then I realized that God's word is for everyone. This woman's brother passed away and left behind five children. She lived in a very small house and, of course, she was not in the position financially to take care of all five children. So, the state only awarded her the two smallest children. One day, she decided to write down on a piece of paper the amount of money she believed she would win. She learned to do this from watching her mother. She wrote down on a piece of paper $112 million, and then she put it underneath her pillow.

In Habakkuk 2:2-3 the word of God says, *Write the vision, and make it plain upon tablets, that he may run that readeth it. For the vision is yet for an appointment time, but at the end it shall speak, and not lie: through it tarry, wait for it; because it will surely come.* God's word is for all people who will receive it, believe it and claim it for themselves. It's for the just and the unjust. The word of God is universal. It is for anyone who will take ownership of it. In her interview, she told the reporter that she's been a giver since she was a little girl. She listed several organizations to which she regularly donates. She said that she believes giving is very important. However, she never said anything about giving praise and honor to God, or being a believer. Still, I concluded that this woman knows how to tap into kingdom principles.

She won $112 million in the lottery. Her story blew my mind! I am not glorifying the lottery, nor am I telling you to go play the lottery. It doesn't matter who you are: just or unjust, black or white, yellow or green. What really matters is how we apply the word of God to our situations. Faith is a free gift that was given to mankind; it shows no favoritism. However, I believe believers get to live in the fullness of God's blessing, according to Deuteronomy 28:1-14. Those of us who have received Christ as Savior get to spend eternity with our Father. The unjust are faced with death as the wages of their sins. Believers get to live on the streets of gold and worship our Savior for eternity. The righteous get to enjoy kingdom benefits because they are citizens of Heaven. These benefits are already made available because of what Jesus on the cross. They include